DUNDY COUNTY BABE

Congratulations Julie,

Verne Stout
aug. 2006

Elsieforne V. Stout

Bloomington, IN   authorHOUSE™   Milton Keynes, UK

AuthorHouse™
1663 Liberty Drive, Suite 200
Bloomington, IN 47403
www.authorhouse.com
Phone: 1-800-839-8640

AuthorHouse™ UK Ltd.
500 Avebury Boulevard
Central Milton Keynes, MK9 2BE
www.authorhouse.co.uk
Phone: 08001974150

First published by AuthorHouse   7/6/2006

ISBN: 1-4259-2423-9 (sc)

Library of Congress Control Number: 2006902578

Printed in the United States of America
Bloomington, Indiana

This book is printed on acid-free paper.

This book is dedicated to victims of abuse, especially verbal abuse.
"Sticks and stones can break your bones; but
words can't hurt you." (Anonymous)
Sticks and stones can break bones which wounds the physical body.
But words can destroy the soul.

BOOKS

My Pioneer Ancestors

ACKNOWLEDGEMENTS

I want to thank my daughter, Ruth Ann Holman, and friends, Marian Battenhouse, Pauline Caldwell, Wynona Springer, Ann Schechter, and Evelyn Gladding for their help in editing these stories. Many thanks to my many friends who have read my book and offered encouragement and support to continue when it seemed easier to forget my dream. With God's help it has been possible to create these events of my life into stories for this book.

AUTHOR'S NOTE

Some of the names in this book have been chosen to protect the identity of the persons I met during my journey from birth through grade school at District #37; high school days at Parks High, Parks, Nebraska; college days at McCook Junior College, McCook, Nebraska; Hastings College, Hastings, Nebraska; life at Sterling College, Sterling, Kansas; teaching days in one-room schools in Nebraska and my marriage and life in Indiana.

TABLE OF CONTENTS

PART III

HIGH SCHOOL

PART IV

COLLEGE – TEACHING

INTRODUCTION

This collection of stories in my life recalls events as I grew up in Dundy County in southwestern Nebraska. This area in Nebraska was part of the Great Plains that the earliest settlers called the "The Great American Desert." Since there were few streams and trees, sandy soil with very little rainfall, this semi-arid area did not meet the earliest settlers' expectations. To these settlers this land was uninhabitable. Many continued to travel westward in their search for rich farmland.

The government offered a homestead **free land**. This offer permitted the settlers to claim land, live on it, improve it, and in five years apply for ownership. However western Nebraska was not a paradise these settlers expected, instead homesteading challenged them with a life filled with hardships and heartaches before ownership could be achieved.

Nature's obstacles for these eager new settlers included: lightning that started prairie fires which burned the grasslands and homes; the searing hot summer temperatures that burned the crops, and severe hail storms that pounded the crops into the ground. (Many times I walked barefooted on the hot sand in summer. At first the sand felt cool, but in seconds my feet felt like I was standing on a hot stove.) Less than 15 inches of annual precipitation resulted in droughts and wind-driven dust storms that depleted the soil; swarms of grasshoppers feasted on crops; and the frigid winter temperatures were accompanied by several severe blizzards each season. The temperature was 35 below zero the day I was born. Indeed only very rugged, brave, determined individuals survived nature's wrath and the economy of the times. The homesteaders had no conveniences. Many people lost their homesteads.

These incidents and stories relate some of the challenges and hardships I endured as I lived differently, like the daughter of a pioneer family, while residing in a more modern world. During this era (1920s-1930s) the evolution in agriculture began with the combining of small farms into larger farms. This transformation enabled the farmers to emerge from pioneer-homesteading with horse-drawn farm equipment era into modern culture with tractors, conveniences, and privileges enjoyed in the East. Rural Electrification did not bring electricity to this part of Nebraska until the early 1950's.

The homesteaders faced many severe challenges in Nebraska. Today those severe conditions have become less problematic with modern inventions. Two determined homesteaders who endured the harsh environment in the early

1900's were my parents: Lydia Grams and Ellis Blamford Mendenhall. I will include a brief history of each of their lives before they become homesteaders in Nebraska.

* * *

Mike Grams, Mama's father, my grandfather, a German emigrant from Prussia, immigrated with his family to Canada. He was dissatisfied with the long, bitter, cold Canadian winters. So he moved his family south to northern North Dakota. Again the winters were still too cold, and then he moved his family to Salisbury, Missouri. My mother, Lydia and her little sister, Emma, were born here. After my grandfather's wife, Eva, died in 1893, he was left with two sons and four daughters: Matilda, the oldest, age 14, went to live with a relatives in Canada; Susan, age seven; Lydia, my mama, three and half; and Emma, their six-month-old baby sister were all sent to live with their Aunt Caroline and her husband, Jacob Wentland in Carrington, North Dakota. Aunt Caroline was Grandma Eva's sister. Uncle Jacob and Aunt Caroline had no children. Grandpa's two sons, Andy and Charles remained with him; in 1902 they moved to western Nebraska and staked a claim for a homestead.

Uncle Jacob chose Mama, age three and a half, to herd cattle on foot on the open range. He believed children should be horse whipped if they made any mistakes. Mama frequently recalled many whippings with a horse whip and was stabbed in the head with a pitch fork. Scars on her scalp verified puncture wounds. Her sister, Susan was kept in the house to help Aunt Caroline and to care for baby Emma.

Aunt Susan, unknown to her aunt or uncle, slipped a letter to Grandpa, Mike Grams, telling him of the cruelty that Uncle Jacob was inflicting on my mama. Grandpa, now a homesteader in Nebraska, went to North Dakota. When he arrived, he found his young daughter thinly clad on horseback herding cattle in a blizzard. He put her into his wagon, and took off his overcoat and put it around her before he talked with Uncle Jacob. Grandpa took my mama to his Nebraska Homestead.

Mama said she never knew how old she was as birthdays were never celebrated by her aunt and uncle. Research revealed that she lived in North Dakota at the time of the 1900 census; she was nine years old and she was listed as a "ward" of her aunt and uncle. (Her sister, Susan was listed as a "ward" while Emma was listed as a niece.)

Her father homesteaded in 1902 and applied for citizenship in 1903. He was declared a citizen in 1908 and could file a claim for ownership of his homestead. Mama was probably 11 years old when she became the housekeeper and cook for Grandpa and her two brothers, Andy and Charles.

Grandpa's homestead was a mile south of the Rollwitz School. It was here that Mama began her first days in school.

It was fortunate that Grandpa took Mama when he did. Mama's youngest sister, Emma was rounding up the cattle on horse-back, and accidentally rode through a slough. The horse became mired in the gummy muck of the slough. Uncle Jacob whipped Emma until she died from the attack in 1905.

* * *

Grandpa Grams married Fredericka Keyser, a mail order bride whose ship passage was paid by grandpa, from Germany in 1908. Fredericka was unhappy with her new husband's daughter in the home. Fredericka loved to crochet. My mama said she wanted to learn to crochet, so she would pick up her step-mother's work to examine it. This made her step-mother angry. Fredericka demanded that Grandpa kick out his daughter. Fredericka had brought her baby daughter Ella with her when she left Germany. Mama was homeless until another homesteader, Teresa Shrum, a young widow with three young children, welcomed her and other homeless youth into her home. Nothing was ever mentioned about Uncle Andy and Uncle Charles; they may have left home.

* * *

Ellis Blamford Mendenhall, my father, was born near Norton, Kansas in a sod house on his parent's homestead. Later the family moved to Iowa. My dad's asthma became a problem in the damp climate in Iowa. After five years, he decided to follow the call "Go west, young man, to find your fortune." He started this journey and worked as he traveled westward. When he reached Dundy County, Nebraska, the drier climate was less irritating for his asthma. Free Land! Stake a claim! What a bargain! My father became a homesteader and staked a claim for a quarter of land about four miles west of Rollwitz in Dundy County. He said, "I never did make it to California."

Dad's homestead had very sandy soil and unsuitable for farming. After he and Mama were married, they sold the homestead and purchased a farm that was owned by Uncle Andy. It was four miles east of Rollwitz. This farm was my birth place and home for 21 years.

* * *

Rollwitz was a small pioneer village organized by my Great Aunt Ernestine Grams Rollwitz, my Grandpa, Mike Grams' sister, and her husband, Adolph. They were homesteaders who saw a need for supplies and a post office closer than Parks which was an 18 mile, two day, journey with a team and wagon. There were two blacksmith shops, a post office, a school with grades 1-10, and a church. Rollwitz today is a town in memory. The location is marked with a large gravestone on which is engraved the names of pioneers who were buried in the Rollwitz church cemetery. All the original cemetery stones have been gone for years.

PART I

PRE-SCHOOL YEARS

MY EARLIEST MEMORIES

Brothers! They can love you and make you feel important, and then can be ornery when they choose you as their subject for a prank. I was the frequent subject of my older brother Alvin's tricks and jokes.

Alvin had stopped to visit at the farm. We chatted in the driveway near the yard gate. "Sis," he called as I started to walk towards the house. I stopped and turned to look at him. "Sis, come here," he beckoned with his hand. What mystery did he forget to reveal? I silently questioned as I walked back where I had left him. "What prank does he have in mind?" I was almost afraid to trust Alvin as he always had some silly trick "up his sleeve" but I returned to the stand near him.

"Look, Sis," he commanded, looking up as he laid his hand on my right shoulder with his finger pointing towards my nose. I knew I dared not turn my head to look him in the eye as my nose would bump his finger, a favorite trick of his. "Look up! See that grasshopper setting on the windmill's tail. He just winked at you!" he chuckled.

I caught my breath as my face turned crimson down to my toes. I was so shy at age 13 that to hear that anyone had winked at me embarrassed me. I felt like hitting him. But I dared not because I'd hear Mama's words, "You sinned against God when you hit your brother." Before I could leave, he chuckled as he quickly repeated, "Sis, he winked at you again." Disgusted, I left immediately for the house.

No one could have seen a full grown grasshopper sitting on that windmill's tail at least 30 feet above us. The windmill, which pumped our water, was currently not running as the stock tank was full on this windless August day. Oh, Brothers!

* * *

Years later, Alvin had stopped at my home in Milroy, Indiana for a quick visit after he had attended a farm machinery seminar in Wisconsin. He and I chatted when he posed the question, "Did you know I taught you to drink milk"? Puzzled, I looked at him as he related this story:

> "You were around one year old. Mama wanted to wean you; she tried to teach you to drink milk but you refused. You cried day and night; you were too hungry to sleep. When Mama worked in the kitchen she'd put you on her bed in the bedroom and expected you to go to sleep. But you were so hungry that you'd crawl to the edge of the bed and cried even louder. Mama walked to her bed; picked you up from the edge then tossed you back towards the wall to the other side of the bed.
>
> I could not bear to hear you cry day and night as I knew you were hungry. One evening I put some milk into a cup, picked you up, and took you to the mirror. I said, 'Watch the baby drink.' As you looked in the mirror, I put the cup to your lips, tipped it to get a little milk on your lips, and after you tasted the milk you wanted more. It was wonderful when you quit crying day and night!"

He was my hero then.

* * *

Alvin and Lyle frequently stopped at home after they had established their trucking business. I heard them ask for "operating money." I was too young to understand why they needed "operating money" but they always received some of Mama's egg money.

One time when Alvin visited, he had a bad fever blister. I don't know if he knew the blisters were spread by kissing or not but he kissed me hard on the mouth. He was always talking about giving me his "cooties."

The following week I had a horrible fever blister that covered my entire upper lip clear up to my nose. One big crusty scab! He was visiting again and kept making wise-cracks to make me laugh. Laughing was so painful. He thought that was funny. I didn't think very much of his humor.

* * *

When Valentine's Day came, Alvin brought me a nice Valentine. It was a blue heart with white lace imprints around the edges, four inches high and six inches across and a half inch thick folded. When the cardboard backings were attached together in the back, it formed a red honey-combed heart with a little girl and boy standing at the gate of a colorful flower garden. The penciled price on the back was twenty-five cents. What a very special "cootie" for him to share with his little sister!

*   *   *

Another time, Mama and I, a young teen, visited him when he was living in the house Mama had built for Alvin and Lyle to live in while they attended high school in Benkelman. He didn't feel well and was eating an apple—then gave it to me. He had the German measles. I fooled him—I never caught his germs and never had the German measles. For once I had the last laugh!

*   *   *

I was between two and three years old when my brothers and I were in the horse barn. I do not recall why, but I remember being lifted up, and laid on my tummy over the manager rail. My panties were pulled down. Lyle relieved his sexual desires by working his penis back and worth between my legs just touching my crotch. The motion rubbed my tender skin raw. There was no penetration. And Alvin? He stood by watching. I could still kick each of them hard for their actions.

Later, everyone was in the kitchen and Mama was giving me a bath. I lay on her lap spread-eagle in my birthday suit with my modesty exposed. She discovered the molestation, and then she yelled at my brothers as I lay there completely exposed. I was so embarrassed.

*   *   *

When I was a toddler, around the age of two, I had a little red three-wheeled, wooden, kiddie car that I loved to push with my feet. Our yard was sandy and I pushed it everywhere. My brothers and my dad were making repairs to the fruit cellar located about 20 feet from the back door of the house. The cement-covered dirt roof leaked, the wooden steps that lead down to the cement floor had decayed, and the slanted stairway door had missing boards. They were busy making the needed repairs.

I loved my little red chariot and had pushed myself near the cellar door to watch the work in progress. Then I jumped off my kiddie car and ran into the house for a drink of water. A few minutes later when I returned, I saw something foreign on the seat of my kiddie car that was black, ugly, and strange; it didn't move. I was frightened. I screamed as loudly as I could.

Mama came running. "What have you guys done to her now?" She yelled as she met me retreating.

Just then, Alvin stepped over to my kiddie car, picked up that "thing" and innocently said, "Look, Sis, it is just an itty, bitty, baby, garter snake. Look, it is dead! It can't hurt you!"

Mama looked at him and sternly scolded, "You should be ashamed of yourself." She and I disappeared into the house leaving many silent snickers. Alvin was such a jokester.

Brothers can be so loving and caring one minute but . . . . Oh! Brothers what horrible memories they can leave! Sometimes!

THE DAY OF MY BIRTH

(While I personally cannot recall the sequence of happenings on the day of my birth, the facts that had been mentioned by Mama combined with information obtained through research are woven into the following tapestry.)

The cold north wind howled as it whistled and swirled around the small, dark, clapboard house that set at the base of the large prairie hill. A few scatterings of snowflakes in the air were forerunners of the approaching blizzard. The animals in the barns near the small house were all quietly sleeping, waiting the dawning of the new day in this southwestern Nebraska home. The icy cold had penetrated into the house until it froze the water in the teakettle that set on the cold kitchen range. No one stirred but snored in their cozy, warm, double beds, in the one and only bedroom.

Mama started to move but stopped to catch her breath as another severe pain hit. "Ellis, it is time to go call the doctor," she cried. She slept on the side of the bed nearer the wall and couldn't get out of bed without crawling over him.

Dad grunted, but remained silent in the cozy, warm bed next to Mama. He could smell the cold, and heard the cold wind whistling. He dreaded to get up or even open his eyes. He began to stir. Oh! How he hated to put his feet on the icy cold, painted wooden floor! Finally, he quickly threw back the quilts, put his feet on the floor and grabbed his socks that lay nearby. He pulled on his cold-chilled socks, overalls, and shirt as he shivered in his long underwear before he made his way into the cold, dark kitchen.

He lit the kerosene lamp that set on the table, filled the firebox of the kitchen range with corn cobs, and topped them with two coal oil-soaked cobs. He lighted a match, dropped it on the cobs, which quickly began to blaze. More cobs were added and soon heat began to radiate out into the room. He stepped to the sink, opened the sliding window to the water room water barrel, and dipped fresh water into the teakettle. The *Benkelman Post,* the weekly county newspaper reported the temperature had dropped to 35 degrees Fahrenheit below zero.

He shrugged into an extra shirt, another pair of overalls, and a sweater, then high-topped leather shoes and four-buckle overshoes. After he topped his garments with the brown cowhide overcoat, tan hunting cap with the fur-lined earflaps, he lit the lantern. Then he grabbed his heavy mittens to the complete protection against the cold, turbulent weather. He headed out into the dark, blustery night with the lantern to light his way to the barn.

Quickly he harnessed the horses and was on his way to the Lutz home two miles away. He saw a few snowflakes swirl in the air. How angry he felt as he remembered when they had had a telephone. He recalled that Andy had called this past Halloween night. Mama had answered the phone, and heard "Boo!" She had recognized her brother, Andy's voice, slammed down the receiver, and cancelled the telephone service.

Mama remained in her bed and called to her two sons, Alvin, age 11 and Lyle, age 9, who slept in the other double bed. They were so comfortable in dreamland but Alvin sleepily responded with a grunt while Lyle continued to snore softly.

A little later Mama got up and shook the boys. "Com' on and git up!" she demanded. "Your dad's gone for the doctor. We need heat in this freezin' room. Alvin, git up and git a fire goin' in this heatin' stove. We need hot water; you can fill the cannin' kettle with water to heat on the stove. The baby's clothes need to be got'en out of the trunk in the front room. Com' on, now. Move! Both of you!" Then she returned to her warm bed as another pain hit.

Slowly Alvin braved the icy chill as he quickly slid his warm feet into his icy-cold socks and pulled his britches up over his long underwear. He shivered as he lit the small lamp that set on the bedroom dresser and started a fire in the little heating stove. He added more fuel to the fire in the kitchen range.

Alvin realized that Lyle was still snoring in their warm bed. "Hey, Lazy Bones!" he teased as he quickly yanked the quilts off his sleeping brother. "Git up and git your britches on and help! You're no better than me." After Lyle lost the warm quilt tug-o'-war, unwillingly he got up and dressed. Together they finished the requested tasks. "Isn't this excitin'?" Alvin exclaimed. "I can hardly wait until my baby brother or sister arrives." Lyle grumbled silently as he knew he would no longer be the baby of the family.

Dad returned and reported, "A storm's brewin', that bitter cold wind's a bringin' a blizzard. Dr. Lewis said he'd be here as quickly as he could. Boys, its early but let's git out after the chores, maybe we'll git done before this blizzard gits any worse. Your mom won't be doing' chores today." Soon they were off with lighted lanterns to milk the cows, feed the cattle, hogs, horses, and chickens and replenish the supply of cobs and coal.

They had just finished the chores and had returned to the house, when Dr. Lewis arrived in his new Model T Ford car. As he came into the house, he said, "I'm certainly thankful for this car as that atrocious wind would have made it near impossible for me to come if I only had my trusty ol' horse and buggy. How is Lydia?" With his little black bag, he went to attend to his patient.

Later at 11:30 a.m. a loud lusty cry was heard in the bedroom. The baby had arrived. Shortly afterwards, Dr. Lewis brought the little bundle into the kitchen and announced, "You have a beautiful baby daughter."

Alvin stepped nearer Dr. Lewis to see the tiny bundle. "Can I hold her?" he asked. Dr. Lewis explained how to hold a new baby then handed me to him. "Hi, Sis, open your eyes! I want to see if they are brown like mine. Com' on," he cooed, as he lightly rubbed my cheek with his finger. "What a wonderful New Year's Day gift you are!" he lovingly continued.

Dr. Lewis stepped back into the bedroom, and returned with his black bag. He sat down at the table by the steaming cup of coffee that was waiting for him. He reached into his bag; drew out a certificate, and began to fill in the blanks. He looked at Dad, and asked, "What are you going to name your beautiful daughter?"

Dad silently stared into space and ignored the question. He thought, "If I suggest a name, Lydia will be angry because she didn't git to name this baby. She didn't understand that **he** was the master of the house; she was the servant. No woman was going to tell **him** what to do." He remained silent.

Finally Dr. Lewis stepped back into the bedroom. "Are you ok?" he inquired of Mama. "Have you picked out a name for your daughter?" Mama laid quietly as many thoughts raced through her mind. She thought, "I wanted Lyle's middle name to be 'Mike' for my dad, Mike Grams. Ellis got so angry that he shook his fist at me and told me **he** would do as he pleased and named him 'Lyle John' after his dad, John Mendenhall. If I say anything about naming this baby, a name that he did not want, he'll just shake his fist in my face and threaten me again. I can't handle that now. I will just keep quiet and **keep the peace**."

At last Dr. Lewis reminded everyone that he would have to leave the name blank when he filed the report the next day. He left for the 25-mile drive back to Benkelman in the now raging blizzard.

* * *

As an adult, I recalled that Mama had mentioned several times that her brother, Uncle Andy, had not named his son, Harry, until after he was two years old. And Dick Keyser, her stepbrother, had not named his son, Eldon, until after he was two years old. I became curious to see if that was true for me. I sent for my birth certificate. Sure enough – my birth had been recorded without a name.

I immediately wrote a letter to Mama and questioned her about it. She replied:

> "I didn't have any say in it. I didn't have time; I was busy washin' white clothes. You were named 'Elsie' because Ellis wanted you named after him. Dick Keyser, (Mama's stepbrother), named you 'Ferne' and Marguerite (Dick's wife), named you 'Verline'. I didn't have any say in *it*."

In later letters I was given a different version of my naming. One time she even blamed Dr. Lewis. My naming has remained a mystery.

BLACK BABY

(Mama rarely talked of my escapades. Once she mentioned I had gotten into a bucket of black axle grease. In this story I have tried to illustrate a two-year olds delight with this taboo substance and her mother's reaction.)

Alvin, Lyle, and Dad had concentrated their thoughts on getting the cultivators greased and out into the field to cultivate the corn before the cloudless windless day became a scorcher. The corn was tall enough to be seen above the dirt ridges. No one took time to put the lid on the half used ten-pound bucket of black axle grease but left it in the driveway, and rushed out to the field. The barnyard was quiet except for the crowing of the roosters and clucking of the hens calling to their babies. Even the cattle and baby calves were out in the pasture grazing.

"What a beautiful day for washing!" Mama said, as she prepared to do the laundry after she and I had fed the baby chicks. We came back to the house; I sat down to play in the yard. Mama quickly got the copper wash boiler into the house, set it on the kitchen range then filled it with water. She built a hot cob fire. The baby's clothes had to be boiled.

I had grown tired of playing with my favorite toys – a pan, a lid, and a big spoon, and looked for a new adventure. I toddled out the open yard gate. I saw something new. "What's that? Could it be a new toy?" I thought as I toddled to the open bucket of axle grease. I bent over and touched it. "Oh, this is fun!" I mused as I pressed my little fingers into more and more of the soft, black, shiny stuff. I sat down and started covering my arms and legs with the black, slippery slime. As I smeared my legs, the sand clung to my hands but I did not care, this was fun! There was plenty more of this soft, black, shiny stuff in the bucket.

While the water was heating, Mama began to sort the clothes. She thought, "If I will set my wash and rinse tubs out on the porch, I will not have the mess on the kitchen floor." She began to set the wash tubs on the wash bench on the porch and laid the washboard with lye soap nearby. As she filled the rinse tubs with water, she realized everything was very, very quiet, actually too quiet. She stopped and listened. "Where is that baby?" she questioned. "What is she into now?" Immediately she called and looked around the yard but did not see me.

Into the house she flew! She looked in the kitchen, in the front room, in the bedroom and back to the kitchen. She called as she looked. Not one little peep or happy coo did she hear, not one rattle of my pan. Everywhere silence met her ears. Panic set in when she stepped back outside and saw the open yard gate. "Did she get tangled up in that machinery as the men left? Oh, I pray she did not toddle down to the water tank and climb up the side and fall into the water," she thought as she frantically continued her search. Still she didn't see me. Then she began to run out the yard gate toward the water tank, and dreaded what she might see.

She stopped abruptly in the middle of the driveway. There I sat, next to that open bucket of black axle grease—a very black, greasy, two-year-old who continued to slather the black grease mixed with sand on my face, arms, and legs. My hands were full of grease as I squished it through my little fingers. "Thank God!" Mama said relieved, as she walked towards that little, black, greasy figure. I continued to slather on more of the grease and sand mixture. "What a mess, you are!" she proclaimed as she walked up and disturbed my concentration of play.

She stood still and stared at me. I looked up and said, "Look-ie, Ma-ma, pretty?" as I squished more black, sandy ooze between my fingers and onto my body and clothes.

Mama quickly snapped the lid on that grease bucket, as she said, "A mess! You are a big mess, a great, big, black, greasy, stinky mess! Not pretty at all! You smell like grease. Ugh! How will I ever get you clean?" Then she grabbed me under my arms, held me away from her, and quickly marched into the yard. She popped me down so hard that I batted my eyes. I was away from everything. "Now stay there!" she demanded as she rushed into the house for some rags.

She quickly returned and started with the top layer of sandy grease. Off came my black, greasy, sandy clothes. I calmly continued to squish that warm, black ooze between my fingers until she wiped my hands clean. I'd tasted it. "Yuck!" I cried and spit it out as Mama cleaned my face and mouth again.

"Serves you right for getting into that grease." she said, as she cleaned and cleaned and scolded with every stroke of the rags. Finally, I began to look like a respectable baby again and smelled almost human. I protested with cries both for the rough treatment and the loss of my "pretty black ooze." She was much too rough; my fun was ruined!

In the evening after the chores were done, the men came into the house for supper. Mama angrily scolded my dad and my brothers for leaving the open bucket of grease in the driveway. "That bucket of grease is ruined," she roared. "You'll have to throw it away. It has sand mixed in it, thanks to this nosy baby. When I found her, she was covered from head to toe with that black, stinky, grease mixed with sand. It took over an hour to clean her up and her clothes were ruined. I am not sure if I got it all out of her hair."

They were all quiet as they looked down their noses at the food on their plates and continued to eat in silence. After several minutes Alvin, my teaser brother, retorted with a laugh, "I bet that would have been a sight to see. I'd have loved to have seen her." Then he turned to me as I sat near him in my high chair, and asked, "Was that fun to play in that ol' black, grease, Sis?" Alvin received a very stern, cold stare from Mama. Did he laugh silently? Who knows!

MY FIRST BOY FRIEND

Alvin and Lyle were both in the eighth grade for the 1928-29 school year. It was the custom for rural teachers to board with a family living in the school district. My brothers were thrilled when they learned their eighth grade school teacher would be a young man, Mr. Hamilton and he would be living with us for the winter. The teachers were charged a small fee for room and board.

Blizzards were common; we were recovering from the latest storm. The temperature that day was very cold with a strong, northwest wind. Chore time had come and everyone was shrugging into their coats. I grabbed my coat and overshoes, too. I did not want to be left in the house alone. I went to my dad, but he ignored me; my brothers were too busy to be bothered. I went to Mama, but she said, "You should stay in as it is too cold for you to be outside."

I just stood in the middle of the kitchen holding my coat and overshoes with tears pooling almost overflowing my eyes. I tried and tried but my coat would not cooperate; my shoes just would not slip into my overshoes.

Finally—Mr. Hamilton saw my problem; he laid his coat on the kitchen stool and said, "Bring your coat and overshoes here, I'll help you." I did as asked. I felt so happy inside. I had found a kind friend. He helped me get bundled up for the cold weather; I went outside for a brief time. I felt so privileged to have found a kind helpful friend and from that day on, Mr. Hamilton was this four-year-olds "boy friend." He was my knight of honor, a very special person, my boy friend.

* * *

Mama chuckled as she recalled this incident:

> "Several weeks later after Christmas vacation, you sat on the kitchen floor playing with your string of play beads. You'd stretch them out the length of your little arms. Mr. Hamilton had just come into the kitchen; he stepped near you to observe your play. He immediately pulled off his bow tie and stretched it to be a little longer than your beads. Then he said, 'My tie is longer than your beads.'"

She continued,

> "You sat there and looked at him and then back at the beads and tie, then said. "But mine doesn't stretch!"

Chuckling again, she said, "You told him good!"

BARBED WIRE GATE

"Want a ride in the car? I'm going check the water in the stock tank in the northwest pasture." Dad stated. I was always ready for an adventure and immediately climbed into the 1924 Model T Touring car beside him. The air was fresh and cool. We arrived at the gate that was located in the slight slope that led to the valley where the well was located. Gates were placed where fewer sagebrush and soap weed (yucca) clumps grew. The hard rain of the night before had washed deeper ruts in the sandy road especially the wheel tracks that led to the well.

Dad drove near the gate, stopped the car, and got out to open the barbed wire gate. He left the motor running, but neglected to pull the hand brake. He started to walk towards the gate but when he was about even with the front of the car; it started to roll forward down the slope of the road. Immediately, he jumped in front of the car, spread out his arms, and pushed against the car with all his strength as he braced his feet in the soft wet sand trying to stop the car from rolling into the gate. The weight of the car with the running motor continued to push forward down the slope and pressed his back tight against the four-strand barbed wire gate.

He screamed, "Put your foot on the brake! Turn the motor off! Turn the key! Stop the car!" I was so frightened, as a four-year-old, I had no idea what he wanted me to do as riding in the car was a rare treat. Fear seized me even more as I saw him red-faced in the spread-eagle position being pushed tighter and tighter against the gate. (That scene is still vivid today.) Finally, I did something to kill the motor, I don't know what, nor do I recall how he got out of that horrible position. Afterwards he pulled the hand brake, opened the gate, and then released the hand brake to let the car roll forward to a level area where he could start the car with the hand crank.

He checked on the water in the stock tank, and the salt block for the cattle then we returned home. He had to tell Mama what happened because his shirt was torn from the many barbs that had gouged deeply into his back. She yelled at him, "What a stupid thing for you to do! Elsieferne could have been killed!" I do not know if she treated his back or not.

His reply was, "I did not want to risk getting a broken arm to start the **** car again with that ***** crank!" as he walked out of the house.

SCOTTSBLUFF

Mama had suffered ill health for months. Her spiritualist papers listed locations where the spiritualists lived and provided healing. One article proclaimed the healing powers of "Dr. Charlie," as people called him, but he was not a medical doctor. An article in the 1951 *Denver Post* stated:

> ". . . Charles McKinnon said his diploma was from heaven. At the age of 12 he was ill. He related. . . three angels came to bear me to heaven. One of them said, 'Let's

leave him on earth as a healer.'" McKinnon continued "I've been healing ever since. . . ."

Information under a photo stated, "McKinnon waved his hands around the patient's head—mean while asking the sufferer to concentrate on 'feeling the breeze.'"

My memories of our stay in Scottsbluff that summer included: living in one room of a large house with other people, viewing the site of a plane crash, shopping at the five and dime store, climbing the Scottsbluff bluff, playing with a little girl, and a big box of hats with shiny pennies. And Mama being sick in bed.

Many years later, I began to wonder about my memories of Scottsbluff; were they real or a dream. One day I asked Alvin, if he remembered Mama and me going to Scottsbluff. "Yes," he said, "I remember," with anger in his voice, as he continued, "Mama took off during spring farm work! We had the cultivating, haying, and other farm work and chores to do plus 'batch' (When men had to do their own cooking, they always called it 'batching'.) You know all farm work was done with manpower (us) and horsepower. There were the chores to do, too. You know how it was then, Sis." He continued "We couldn't take off like Mama did."

Mama did not trust medical doctors but she felt that Charles McKinnon or Dr. Charlie, the "spiritual healer" could heal her. The paper stated that he was located in Scottsbluff, Nebraska and he sounded like a miracle healer. He did not charge fees but accepted donations. She wanted that miracle, too. She began to plan to go to Scottsbluff to be healed.

Dad took a day off from spring work to take Mama and me to Scottsbluff in our 1924 Model T Ford touring car. The roads were narrow, unpaved dirt with some sections covered lightly with gravel.

In Scottsbluff, Mama rented a room on the first floor, near the front door of the large rooming house. Our room was furnished with a double bed, a small table with two chairs, a single burner, gas hot plate, food storage cabinet, a small icebox, and hooks on which to hang our clothes. A small, bare, ceiling light bulb and a small south window provided light. The first floor residents shared the bathroom at the end of the long hall.

The red brick two-story, half block long building of 50 rooms, was built by the local sugar factory in 1912 as a dormitory for their workmen. After it was no longer needed as a dormitory, it was turned into a rooming house, than was vacant for years. Today it has been restored and again it is a rooming house for low-income people.

We walked everywhere in Scottsbluff. Near the time of our arrival, a plane crashed in the street a few blocks from the rooming house. We walked to the site; there was an awesome, huge, black crater in the center of the street with fire-scorched, jagged, brown edges. The siding of the nearby houses showed signs of scorch as well as the leaves on the trees in the adjacent yards. All signs of the wrecked plane were gone. A plane crash—I just couldn't picture an airplane on the ground as all the planes I had seen were flying high overhead.

The Scottsbluff newspaper, *The Star-Herald*, carried the story of the plane crash on June 2, 1930. It was a two-passenger cloth-bodied plane that had left Kearney, Nebraska about 4 p.m. and was to arrive in Scottsbluff about an hour later. The two passengers, officials of the Western Public Service Company were enroute to a conference in Scottsbluff. It was suspected that the gas tank exploded in the air causing the plane to burst into flames. The flaming plane struck a school and a store before it plummeted into the street. Air travel was in its infancy at this time. I had wondered how old I was when we were in Scottsbluff, but when I read that article I discovered that I was just five years old.

On the farm, Mama used lard to fry foods with heat provided by a cob and coal fire; here she had a one-burner, gas hot plate. After she used all the lard she had brought with us, she purchased corn oil. The gas hot plate provided a hotter fire so when she cooked with the corn oil a most unpleasant, horrible odor filled the room. I dreaded meal times.

When the butter Mama had brought from the farm was gone, she purchased oleo. It was all white with a small capsule of yellow food coloring in the package. The coloring was to be blended into the oleo. It still tasted more like lard than butter. It was "Yuck"! The oleo was cheaper to buy than the creamery butter.

She and I walked the eight or nine blocks downtown many times. We frequently stopped at the five and ten cent store. In the center of the store, near the doorway, was the large, square, candy counter where bulk candy was sold. Like all children, I began walking around the counter looking at all the mouth-watering, colorful sweets. Naturally, I asked Mama to buy me some candy. As we walked past the counter one day, Mama noticed the opening to the inside area of the display counter. No clerks were in sight. She said, "You can go in (that opening); if you find candy on the floor; you can have it, as the store wouldn't want it. They'd just throw it away." She reminded me that she had no money to buy candy; also, candy was not good for me! I did find a few pieces of unwrapped candy which I picked up and ate.

I do not recall if Mama ever saw the faith healer, Dr. Charlie. According to records, he didn't live in Scottsbluff but had resided in Gering, Nebraska, a small town three miles from Scottsbluff during 1930. I do not recall that we walked that far, but I do recall her being ill with mumps. Someone, perhaps a doctor, came to our room once to check on Mama. She was ill in bed for many days.

I played with a little girl, who lived in the rooming house. We stayed outside near the front door. One day a well-dressed older lady, a second floor resident, brought out a big box of hats. She said, "You girls can play with these." What fun it was to play with those pretty hats! When we got to the bottom of the box, we found several shiny pennies. Immediately we ran upstairs with the pennies and showed them to the kind lady, who said, "You can keep the pennies". I was delighted as I rarely had any money!

We stayed in Scottsbluff over three months. Dad again left the farm in charge of Alvin and Lyle, and came to bring us home in August. Grandpa Mendenhall and Grandpa's sister, Great Aunt Mary, from Lincoln, Nebraska had come to the farm to visit. They followed Dad to Scottsbluff to see the sights. We all drove out to see the big, brown, sandstone bluff that was west of the city. The bluff was discovered and named by Hiram Scott, an explorer and employee of the Rocky Mountain Fur Company.

This bluff, over 900 feet tall, was part of the beginning foothills of the Rocky Mountains, and could be seen for many miles. Mama, Dad, and I started to walk up the newly built zig-zagged path. It was so challenging that Mama turned around when we were about half way to the top and said she could not make it. She returned to the cars and joined Grandpa and Great Aunt Mary as they watched Dad and I walk to the very top of the bluff.

I was impressed! To the west, I could see down the bare west side of the brown bluff and in the distance many evergreen trees. "That is the state of Wyoming" I heard someone say. To the east, north, and south, I could see the town of Scottsbluff, surrounded by pastures, fields, and roads. I was happy and proud that I had walked all the way up that tall bluff.

Soon afterwards, we left Scottsbluff for home. The weather had turned cold, windy and rainy. Our car had oilcloth snap-on side curtains with small celluloid windows, but no heater. The curtains helped keep out the wind and rain but not the cold. My dad drove at the top speed of 20-25 miles an hour. After we had traveled for hours, darkness was fast approaching. We needed to find a cabin to spend the night. We soon came to a gas station with several small cabins in a semi-circle around to the back of the station that provided lodging for travelers. The one we rented was furnished with a kerosene heater, a small table with two straight-backed chairs, a kerosene lamp set on the table, a double bed with blankets, a wash stand with a blue enamel wash basin, and a bucket of water. The rest room was out back of the cabins.

I was so very cold and cried, "I'm cold; I'm so cold." My dad tried to light the heater but it refused to provide heat. Instead it gave off a horrible, offensive stink and smoke. We were all very tired and soon went to bed. I slept between my parents in order to get warm.

We headed home early the next morning and arrived in the afternoon. My teenaged brothers were very pleased to have us back home. They had had to do all the chores and cook for themselves while they were alone.

KANSAS CITY, MISSOURI

Was it spring? Or late summer? The weather was pleasant. A light jacket was needed in this "play in the park weather." Mama and I were in a city park, my first visit to a park. "Can I swing?" I begged, as we walked near four high swings. The swings were so high that I needed help to get onto the seat that came almost up to my shoulders as I stood in the hole under the swing, a hole worn from years of wear from many feet in this Kansas City, Missouri Park. Mama lifted me into the seat and pushed me several times. How I loved to swing; the feeling of the cool breeze against my face was heavenly. When I tried to get out of the swing, I fell, bumped my head on the hard dirt, and cried. Mama helped me up then scolded me severely for not being careful; we immediately left the park. What a sad ending to my first heavenly experience in a swing!

We had come to Kansas City, Missouri for Mama to be treated at Dr. Plank's Temple of Health. The article in her "Spiritualist" newspaper described Dr. Plank's healing powers. The Temple of Health, a large stately white building, served as his office and treatment center. Dr. Plank was a man of medium build with white hair and beard, who reminded me of a grandfather. Mama rejected normal treatment from medical doctors but Dr. Plank was different, she believed, because he was a "Spiritualist," a spiritual healer.

Mama's treatment was a blur to me. But I recall that she was put on a strict diet of raw cabbage, plain boiled potatoes with their jackets (skin) on, sour cream, and half a grapefruit daily. She remained on that diet for years. Chewing the raw cabbage was difficult for her, as she had lost all of her molars on one side.

I wasn't sick, but I was put on a breakfast of just one-half cup of stewed tomatoes – reason, "You must let your stomach rest." That was just one of the unusual routines for me, which included: vermifuge daily (the taste "Ugh") that Mama said I needed because I gritted my teeth at night when I was a toddler. The daily vermifuge continued many years and the enemas several times a week with lye-soap suds to "kill all the germs" during my grade school years. And the spring tonic—molasses and sulphur. How did my little body tolerate?

I saw my first movie in black and white in Kansas City. I can still see those little white lambs coming from the top of the screen and hear the tinkling of the small bells hanging on their necks. A man, who Mama had met at the Temple of Health, was allowed to take me. He was kind to me and bought me an ice cream cone on the way back to the Temple.

A lady who resided at the rooming house where Mama and I stayed had a little girl, Phoebe. Phoebe and I often played together. She was two years older than my six years. One night Phoebe stayed with me, while our mamas attended a meeting. I had begged and begged Mama to take me but she said, "No." I believe that meeting was a séance. She likely attended a séance the day I was taken to the movie. Mama had a fascination of wanting contact the "spirits."

Kansas City had a lot of factories and large stores all with coal-burning heating systems that poured billows of soot-filled black smoke into the air. The soot clung to everything: trees, telephone poles, and buildings. One evening as we walked through the alley to the entrance of our rooming house, I accidentally brushed against a pole and immediately I saw my mistake. My lightweight tan jacket had big black streaks on it. Mama scolded me severely as she had no way to wash clothes except in the bathroom sink; the wet clothes had to be hung in our room to dry. I felt badly that I had been so careless. She washed my jacket to prevent the soot from smearing on everything that I touched. The weather was just cool enough that a jacket was necessary.

Many street venders shouted their wares in the streets. One vender cried, "Tamales, hot tamales, hot tamales." One evening on our way back to our room; I again begged, "Can I have a hot tamale?" Finally Mama purchased one for me. The seasoned cornmeal filling was wrapped in cornhusks which tasted very unusual. I sort-of-liked the taste yet I did not like it. The street venders sold ice cream, hot dogs and many other items.

After seven weeks, Mama prepared to leave Kansas City for home. She packed our two large suitcases and began to walk to the bus station. The sidewalk was crowded with many people bustling in all directions. I walked beside her. We came to a street crossing; cars zoomed past with horns blaring. She stepped off the curb as if she were going to cross that very busy street. I'd noticed people had stopped and the light was red. I can't explain why; but I recall that I stepped in front of her and stopped her from trying to cross the street filled with the speeding cars. Those fast-moving vehicles frightened me.

We arrived at the bus station early. I needed to use the rest room. We searched and finally found the room with many stalls, but all the stalls had a lock on the door. In order to open the door, a nickel had to be deposited in the slot lock. However, there was one stall without a lock at the far end of the long room. Mama said, "It's for blacks." A black lady was standing in the large room—watching the people. Mama said, "I have no money; we'll have to wait to use the unlocked stall." She thought it was crazy to have to pay to use a toilet. It was a long wait as a long line of women and girls were ahead of us. This stall, without a lock on the door, had its own unpleasant, distinctive, foul odors. I was so glad when we could board the bus.

We left town on the big Greyhound bus. I said good bye to the city noises, soot covered poles, unpleasant smells, vendor's cries, and to the scary Katz Drug stores' rolling, cat eye neon signs that extended out over the sidewalks. Those eyes, hypnotized me! I just couldn't take my eyes off them. (I understand the Katz Drugs stores are still serving customers now under the name of Osco Drugs.) I snuggled against Mama, closed my eyes and went to sleep. Several hours later we arrived in Lincoln, Nebraska.

LINCOLN, NEBRASKA - SUMMER 1931

As Mama and I traveled home on the big Greyhound bus, we needed to change to a different bus in Lincoln, Nebraska. My dad asked us to stop and visit his father as we came through Lincoln. Mama didn't want to stop, but she said, "We'll stop to **keep peace in the family**."

The next morning after our arrival, Grandpa asked me to accompany him to the nearby grocery store for bread and milk. As we walked to the store, I heard bells chime. "What's that?" I chirped. Soon a long, big, red, low, shiny vehicle rounded the corner as it crept down the middle of the street. It was a strange sight to this little country gal. This long, red, shiny vehicle reminded me of the long, green hornworms we had on the tomato plants in the garden. The street car moved slowly along the steel track located in the middle of the street with its tail sticking up in back, just like a green hornworm's tail. Only the street car's "tail" touched taut wires, which were mounted high over the middle of the street. Wires from the tall poles on each side of the street provided anchors for the center of the street power line.

Grandpa explained that the little bell chimed as the street car moved along to let people know that it was coming and warn them to get out of the way. All this was so new, so strange and mesmerizing to a little country gal that as soon as I saw it; I knew I had to race that car. Silly 'ol me, I took off running as fast as I could. I zipped across the street in the middle of the block right in front of that car with bell clanging. I made it safely to the other side.

I turned around; my heart was pounding. I looked back across the street where Grandpa stood with his mouth agape, standing where I had left him. He stared at his crazy little granddaughter. Grandpa slowly made his way across the street to the store where he purchased the needed groceries. My punishment? Memory fails—after all who would want to remember such things as punishments!? It had been such fun for me. I had raced that street car and had won. I wonder what that driver thought. Mama never mentioned it. My guess is she never knew of my dangerous escapade.

I was able to see Grandpa Mendenhall only three or four times in my life. That was the last time I saw him. He passed away when I was in high school. I'll bet he never forgot this crazy, lively, adventurous granddaughter who lived so dangerously.

The next day, Great Aunt Mary, Grandpa's sister, who took care of the house for Grandpa, persuaded Mama to go shopping to buy herself a nice dress. We went shopping in the big stores. Mama bought a pretty dress that "under the store lights" appeared to be navy blue rayon with colorful flowers. When we got home on the farm, she looked at the dress in daylight and saw it was black with flowers. She hated black. Working on the farm all the time, Mama rarely had an occasion to wear a nice dress. Black, she related, reminded her of death. She wanted to think of life. That dress was worn once or–twice—yes, just to funerals.

I was very happy to get back home to the farm after being away for two months, first in Kansas City, Missouri, then Lincoln, Nebraska. It was cooler on the farm. Here there were no street cars to race, or the constant honking of car horns, or the Katz Drugs' green cat eyes to stare at, or soot-covered posts to avoid.

What pleasure it was to wriggle my toes in the sand again! I had missed hearing the sounds of nature—the night sounds: crickets' chirp and the coyotes' howl, and the day sounds—the birds singing, chickens clucking, cows and calves bawling and pigs grunting. It was a glorious to awaken to the sounds of nature instead of the smelly, sooty, machine sounds of the city. You knew that a bright, new, fresh day was here when you heard the roosters' crow "Good morning, world: This is the new day that God has given us."

My Kiddie car.
A sketch by the Author.

18

Author, age four, told to look at the sun for this photo

My brothers, Alvin holding me atop truck rack, while Lyle sits on the hood of their truck.

PART II

GRADE SCHOOL YEARS

MY FIRST DAY AT SCHOOL

It was a sunny September morning. Mama said, "School starts today. You wear this nice long sleeved brown dress, the new long brown stockings and your new high-topped black shoes." I dreaded the long sleeves, long stockings and shoes. I protested. "It is a sin to show your legs and arms and you need high-topped shoes to support your ankles." Mama replied. Yet all summer I had worn elbow-length sleeves and had gone shoeless without my ankles hurting. Reluctantly, I complied since there was no choice but I thought how much fun it had been going barefooted, wriggling my toes in the warm sand until the little, round, spiny, seed balls of the sand burs ripened and clung to my little bare feet.

"Come 'n, hurry, you don't wanta be late," she commanded as I lingered tying my shoe strings. "Hurry, I have at brush and braid your hair." Half-heartedly I complied, I dreaded sitting on the tall kitchen stool and have my hair pulled as the pin-bristled brush was pulled through my hair scratching my scalp. Mama was never gentle but held tight when I yelled "ouch" or pulled away. She was hurting my head. The pin-bristled brush removed the tangles from my shoulder length hair. It was a dreaded battle every school day. After the brushing routine, my hair was tightly braided into two braids. When the braids were long enough, she wrapped them tightly around my head and secured them with hairpins. Again the pins often scratched my head, as they were hastily put in my hair.

Mama was always in a hurry. She'd talked about school for over a week, telling me that this was my year to go. My two brothers had graduated from the eighth grade District #37, two years before. I asked, "Why do I need to go to school? I can count to 100, write my name and all of my letters and say my A B C's."

"You have to learn to read and to do better," she explained. "Come on, hurry, here's your lunch pail," she said, as she handed me a shiny new syrup pail. "I'll walk part way with you." She picked up two brown penny pencils tipped with tiny erasers, a small box of waxy crayons and a thin 10 cent pencil tablet of rough white paper with blue lines on it as we walked out the door.

We walked across our sand bur filled, cornfield south of the house; then on the sandy road over two very sandy twin hills with barbed wire pasture fences on either side, then across the grassy area at the end of the neighbor's cornfield. As we cut across the dry, dusty, brown, grassy area, Mama explained that this was the route I was to use as I walked to and from school. "You are **never, never** to follow the road because it would not be safe. You must **never, never** accept a ride from anyone."

When the little white schoolhouse was in sight, Mama stopped and said, "Here's your pencils, crayons, and tablet; now hurry, don't be late. 'Member you must always to walk home the way we came. **Never, never** follow the road." She turned and left while I pleaded for her to come with me.

After several steps toward home, she stopped, turned around and said, "No, I have work to do. I'm not dressed fit to be seen." I didn't think she looked so bad except her apron was dirty and her hair was uncombed. She turned again and left me standing in the field confused and alone. I looked at the schoolhouse then at her back as she disappeared.

I stood there tightly clutching my things; again I looked where I'd last seen Mama, then again at the school where the happy children ran and shouted as they played. I stood there not feeling joyous but anxious, frightened, abandoned and thought—why couldn't she have left that dirty old patched apron at home? The faded dress did not seem so bad. What can I do? No choice, I will have to go on alone.

I stared at the little white clapboard school and the children in the school yard who sounded so joyful. Suddenly I was more afraid as this was so strange, so foreign, so frightening. I knew no one. Mama was gone. I was alone. Oh! The school bell clanged! Mama's last words came back to me "Don't be late!" The children stopped their play and began to run into the schoolhouse.

I pulled my things closer to my body and began to run, too. I stopped in the school house doorway out of breath. I stood there and looked inside. Everyone sat at a desk. A lady in a pretty flowered blue dress was writing on the large blackboard that covered the entire the wall behind teacher's large wooden desk at the front of the room. To the left, I saw three tall windows; below the windows were a row of desks with two children at each desk. To my right were tall windows with a row of desks like those on left side of the

22

room. In front of me, set a large black pot-bellied stove with a long black stovepipe leading to the chimney at the front of the room and a short row of three smaller desks with only two empty desks left.

When the lady turned around, I saw the soft brown curls that framed her pretty young face; her sweet smile made me the feel that I had met a friend. "Come in," she quickly invited, "You may set your lunch pail on that table with the others. Let's find you a desk. Try this one." she continued as she stepped to an empty desk in the center of the room. Fearfully, I walked to the selected desk and sat down. "Do your feet set flat on the floor?" I nodded my head. "Good, this will be your desk. You may put your tablet, pencils, and crayons in your desk." I did this while I cautiously glanced around and saw the many pairs of eyes that stared at me. I'd heard giggles and snickers; I wanted to run home.

The lady returned to the front of the room, with a warm smile, she said, "I'm Miss Stamn, your teacher. Today is September 7, 1931," as she pointed to her name and the date on the blackboard. "I will need to record your name, age, and birthday in my record book. I'll begin with the little girl in the red dress," she said, as she looked at the blond girl wearing a colorful, short-sleeved, red floral dress in the front row. I thought, "I would love to wear that pretty dress and have my curled hair hang free like hers!"

Miss Stamn sat at her desk writing the name of each child in her book. When my turn came, I just sat there and looked at her. I was too afraid to reply. My eyes pooled as I fought tears. She spoke a name, and asked, "Is that your name?" I nodded my head. Then she wrote in her book.

After the names were recorded, Miss Stamn requested that we all stand, look at our country's flag which was tacked on the wall, to our right, above the big blackboard, and repeat the pledge to our flag honoring our country. "You must hold your right hand over your heart." She informed us, then asked, "Johnny," one of the older boys, "will you lead us in the pledge?" After the pledge, while we were still standing, she said, "We'll sing, 'My Country 'Tis of Thee.' I have written the words on the blackboard." Then she said, "You may be seated."

"We will begin our classes. Students in grades two through eight may come up to my desk to get your reading books. Your assignments are on the board. You may quietly read at your desk while the other classes have recitation time. If you need help, raise your hand, one of the older children can help you." Then she asked the four little girls: Birdena, teacher's little sister, Leanna, Leitha, and me, to come to the long wooden recitation bench setting to the left of her desk.

She smiled and said, "You will start to learn your A B C's: you need to learn the name of each letter and to print them on the blackboard. I have

23

printed a letter on each of these cards." As I looked at the letters, they looked strange because I wrote my letters in unconnected cursive. She continued, "Any letter you miss when we name the letters, you will take that card to your desk. Go to the back of the room to the green, orange crate and get a can of shelled corn from the shelf. Use the corn to outline each letter, repeat the name of the letter softly to yourself as you do this. I will take a time between the other classes to check how many letters you have learned." I spent my time, until recess, outlining the letters with the yellow kernels of corn. The yellow kernels fascinated me, as I'd never seen yellow corn. The corn that we raised was blue or white. While the older classes read, I would sit and listen to the stories as I outlined the letters. When Miss Stamn came to my desk to ask the name of the letters, I never answered her even though I knew the name of each letter.

Morning recess was at 10:00 o'clock. The other children happily ran outside to play while I stood alone in the shade of the schoolhouse. There were no shade trees. It was such a hot day to wear long sleeves, and long stockings with high-topped shoes. I was hot and miserable. The other girls looked so cool and free with their colorful, short-sleeved dresses, knee length skirts and anklets.

The school ground was covered with short stubby weed and grass stalks left after the summer's growth of weeds and grasses had been mowed last week. It was hard to walk or run because of the stalks. I knew no one and no one knew me. I had never played with children. Mama was always busy and she didn't want to visit with the neighbors. There were no children at the homes of our closest neighbors any way. My dad rarely talked to me except to scold me. My brothers were attending high school and lived in Benkelman, Nebraska near their school. I always had to play by myself.

After recess, everyone had arithmetic. Grades two through eight had arithmetic work books furnished by the school. The first graders wrote the numbers on the blackboard. Paper and pencils were too expensive to use for practice work. There were no pencil sharpeners at school. If one of the older boys had a knife, he would be allowed to sharpen the pencils at recess, or the teacher sharpened the pencils before school. I was requested to bring my pencil home to be sharpened.

At noon, we sat outside on the ground in the shade of the schoolhouse to eat our lunch. Most of the other children had syrup pails like mine. I had a sandwich of homemade bread with homemade grape jelly, and a small homemade cookie or a small apple. Many times my sandwich was made with lard and sugar. Some of the other children had sandwiches made with bakery bread. I was very hungry as my breakfast had been just a half-cup of stewed tomatoes. I was thirsty. The teacher had brought water to school, but only the students who had a cup could get a drink. We did not know a cup was needed. Hordes of gnats joined us at lunch; they swarmed in our faces and especially in our eyes. They also tormented us in the school room.

After an hour's break for lunch and playtime, we had grammar and spelling classes. The school provided grammar workbooks for grades two through eight. One or two days a week penmanship for writing was taught except for the first graders who practiced printing letters. I continued writing my letters in unconnected cursive.

Writing was taught using the Palmer method, which was using the whole arm in left and right ovals, and push and pulls. These writing exercises of ovals and push and pulls had to be kept between the lines and were used to prepare for cursive writing. Left-handed students were forced to hold the paper with the top slanted to the left, like the right-handed students did. They learned to write upside down with their left hand held in a very awkward curved position that looked most uncomfortable. One day a week we were given white writing paper to do our best. Grades one through three used pencils while grades four through eight used dip pens and ink. Everyone tried to their best as these papers were graded and the best papers were displayed.

Geography was taught after the last recess. The first grade had another class of reading. I outlined more letters with the corn kernels. After we learned the names of the letters, and wrote them, we were allowed to draw on the blackboard. I was too afraid to talk. I just sat at my seat and listened to the older children recite their lessons.

School was out at four o'clock and was I glad! I could go home! As soon as I was away from the school where no one could see me, I rolled my stockings down to my ankles. What a relief! As I walked through the weedy cornfield, the round, ripe, sticky, sand bur seeds clung to everything and especially to my knitted cotton stockings. Mama was very unhappy about the sand burs in my stockings and made me pick those sticky burs out before I did my chores. They hurt my fingers, too. I was so happy that the first day of school was over.

MY SQUIRREL

Southwest Nebraska had semi-arid climate with very little rainfall. Few trees survived the with little moisture, and the cold, winter winds. Friday afternoon after the last recess was my first art class. Each student was given a picture to color of a squirrel sitting up holding a nut between its paws. I'd never seen a squirrel.

I made my squirrel very dark, shiny brown. All 32 squirrels were displayed on the classroom walls. I was very proud of my squirrel and thought it was the best-colored squirrel. I was so anxious to show Mama; I wanted to make her happy and to be proud of me—to love me; it felt horrible when she pushed me away with her arm!

When the squirrel pictures were returned, we took them home. I held my squirrel picture and other papers tightly in my hand as I walked home from school. A brisk west wind was blowing. As I rushed across our harvested corn field through the rows of broken corn stalks, I tripped and fell. I dropped my papers. I cried as I searched through the broken corn stalks for my papers that had been scattered by the wind. I could not find my large beautiful squirrel and began expounding loudly all of the four-letter words that I had heard uttered by the men at home—my dad, my brothers, and the hired men.

I kept searching among the criss-crossed broken corn stalks getting near to the east pasture fence. Then all of a sudden I realized I heard a nearby voice saying, "How sinful you are to curse God. He didn't lose your squirrel picture. You have sinned against God." I felt my face flush in embarrassment like I'd been caught doing something very wrong. I didn't know where the voice came from but it was very real.

I sobbed, "Forgive me, God," as I pulled my dress tightly around my body so I could crawl under the barbed wire fence to search in the pasture. I was hoping I would not tear my dress. With over flowing eyes, the tears formed rivulets and washed the dust from my face. I looked among the clumps of sagebrush and soap weed (yucca) clumps. I felt sorry I had been so sinful. Then almost like magic, I spied that picture lying on the sharp spiny leaves of a soap weed clump, like I was led to it. I quickly picked up my picture and rushed to get out of the pasture. I had been told never to walk in the pasture as there was danger—the cattle could chase me; and rattlesnakes could be hidden around the sagebrush and the yucca clumps. I quickly escaped as I carefully crawled under the fence again. I was afraid that the cattle might instantly appear even though none were in sight.

Whenever I see a squirrel today, I recall how this incident changed my life. There was no church to attend. Mama read from the New Testament once in a while without explanations. The words she read had no meaning for me, and I am not sure how much she really understood as she had very little education.

I believe Jesus walked with me in that field. I am reminded of my favorite song: "I come to the garden alone, while the dew is still on the roses. . . ." Now I have changed it to: "I walked in the field alone, while the sand burs reach to grab me, but Jesus was there when I felt lost and alone. . . ." I felt that He was with me. His guardian angel was always nearby when I need help. I was so thankful.

MY FIRST CHRISTMAS TREE

Just five more days of school, then Christmas vacation! Great! Then, I'll not have the one and half-mile walk in the cold and snow for a few days. I looked forward to my first Christmas vacation and my seventh birthday.

As I walked into my school room that Monday morning, the sight at the front of the room surprised me. No, it enthralled me! Behind our recitation bench, stood a great, big, beautifully, decorated evergreen tree, the first Christmas tree I'd seen. It was so gorgeous it almost took my breath away. I just stood there drinking in the beauty, and absorbing the wonderful cedar aroma that filled the room.

The full, dark, green branches were swirled with garlands of shiny, silver tinsel, white popcorn, and ruby red cranberry strings. Shimmering tin foil icicles dripped from the branches that were tipped with miniature unlighted candles. Many glistening glass balls of red, green, yellow, blue, gold and silver were hung throughout the branches. The tips of the branches were frosted with light airy whiffs of white angel hair making it look like Jack Frost had lightly kissed each branch and left his icy breath of tiny threads of brilliant silver. A dazzlingly beautiful angel adorned in a heavenly white robe, trimmed in gold, reigned in all of her glory at the very top of the tree. To this small girl, the stunning tree appeared to be 15 feet tall but I doubt that it was more than eight feet.

I could hardly wait to get home that night to tell Mama about it. Also, the other children were talking about Santa Claus coming to town on Saturday. I said, "I want to go see Santa Claus when he comes to town on Saturday afternoon." I was so excited. I just could not stand still while I told Mama my exciting news.

Mama was unimpressed about the tree. She said, "Santa is just something made up; he isn't real; he's just a man dressed up in a red suit." What disappointment! I felt sad. I did not really understand her words as the other children were so excited about seeing Santa. It sounded like a most fantastic event. Now I would not get to experience that excitement. I felt Mama didn't love me. My enthusiasm for Christmas was smashed. I wanted to see this Santa and did not care if he was just made up.

On Friday afternoon just before our vacation, we had our gift exchange after the last recess. We had drawn names earlier in December. I had the name of Willis, a boy a year older than me. Mama said we had no money to buy a gift so she took a pair of my new long brown cotton stockings and said "These will be good enough." She helped me wrap them in plain brown paper. All the other gifts were wrapped in brightly colored paper. Willis was angry with his gift. He was so enraged because he received girl's stockings that he tried to put his dirty shoe into my lunch box while I was eating lunch when we returned to school after Christmas vacation. He sneered at me for giving him "girl's stockings." I was confused and sad. I had given him the only gift I had to give. Mama said that we could not buy a gift because we had no money. Actually that was the only new pair of stockings I had. In the fall, Mama had given me a dozen eggs to take to the store to trade for the stockings. We were like many of the people of that era – no money.

We never had Christmas gifts at home. No Christmas tree and no hanging of stockings on Christmas Eve. Mama baked cookies and make candy to go with the baked fat old hen with dressing, home-made noodles, plain boiled potatoes, and green beans. Fat hens no longer laid eggs but ate a lot of feed; they provided food for us.

* * *

I had some happier Christmas memories. The only Christmas gifts I received were from Grandpa Grams, Mama's father, in California and Aunty Susan, Mama's sister, in Montana. Grandpa's box usually contained a small gift for me and some nice warm used clothing from an older lady for me to wear to school, hard candy, nuts, and tangerines. Aunt Susan sent many nice gifts including: perfume, silk stockings, kid gloves, and a set of "Gone with the Wind" handkerchiefs, three new cotton dresses, two beautiful chenille robes, a nice wool blanket, and more.

* * *

One year Uncle Andy brought us gifts before Christmas. My special gift was a demitasse cup and saucer along with gifts for Mama and Dad plus oranges, candy, and nuts. Later Mama used my demitasse saucer in my dad's lunch bucket. One day it came home broken. I cried and voiced my protest. "You had no right to use my saucer; there were other saucers to use." I wailed. She ignored me; she showed that she did not care that my saucer was broken. The unusual thing about these gifts from Uncle Andy was that Mama said, "Uncle Andy's did not celebrate Christmas because they belonged to the Church of Christ." That made the cup and saucer extra special to me; the broken saucer broke my heart.

THE WALK HOME AFTER A BLIZZARD

A blizzard during my first year in school left mounds of snow drifted and sculptured by strong northwest winds as it twirled and swirled the flakes in the frigid temperatures that accompanied the blizzard. The snow had ceased after a day and night of falling, but the icy-wind continued its harsh, cold, razor-sharp breath. Everywhere in the farm landscape were ghostly, white, sculptured drifts. There were no snow days, no school busses, or substitute teachers.

Today was Monday, January 2, school was held as usual. The usual first tasks of the day were the chores. The animals depended on us for food and shelter. My job was to feed and water the chickens which included removing the ice from their water containers; milk my cow, Bessie; and feed six hungry young calves milk from a bucket. The icy-breath of that northwest wind continued to chill bones, and nip the toes, and fingers. I rushed to complete my chores and to get back into the warm house.

The kitchen was the only heated room of our three-room house. As I washed my hands and face and changed into my school clothes, Mama came into the kitchen after she finished milking her cows. She looked at me and said, "You'll have to bundle up real good; it is freezin' cold out. Here, you wear this extra heavy long coat, this extra pair of mittens, and this warm scarf. You don't wanta get cold." She quickly made my lunch and handed me the usual breakfast of a half-cup of hot cooked tomatoes.

With my lunch pail, I started on the one and one-half mile trek to school. I was thankful that wind was at my back as it helped propel me towards the one-room school. And heat! School would start at 9:00 a.m. It was too cold to linger on the way. I rushed as fast as I could through the snow-filled field, over the two snowy, sandy twin-hills, and the snowy grass area at the end of the neighbor's field where I had been instructed to walk. The snow was deeper in the fields because it had drifted in the rows of twisted and bent corn stalks left by the men as the corn was husked. I was tired when I arrived at the warm school to find only a few of the students and the teacher. Many of the roads were drifted full with snow.

Recesses were inside; our favorite inside games included: "Fruit-basket Upset", "Blind Man's Bluff", and "I Spy", and drawing pictures on the blackboard and games like "Tic Tac Toe."

School was dismissed as usual at 4 p.m. Miss Stamn helped me bundle up. How I dreaded the cold walk home facing the razor-sharp wind. I slowly crunched the crisp snow under my feet, a sound I loved to hear, as each step took me closer to home. I had chosen to walk in the road even though I had been forbidden to do that. The snow was not as deep on the road as it was in the fields. I believed that Mama would understand why I chose to walk in the road.

As I walked the quarter mile towards the only house between my home and the school, the home of Frank Graham, an elderly widower, and his daughter, Beulah, I was freezing cold. I started to slowly crunch past their driveway, instead my footsteps automatically turned toward their house as I thought of the warm stove. My long coat made walking slow and more difficult as I plodded through the ice-encrusted snow facing the frosty wind.

I knocked and Beulah immediately welcomed me into the living room with "Come in, take your coat off, and sit by the stove to warm up." Then she stepped into the kitchen and returned with a tasty cup of hot cocoa and two soda crackers on the saucer. What a treat! I had never tasted hot cocoa before. As I relished the delicious drink, I thought about the cold and knew I should not have stopped. But it was so easy to linger in the warm house. Oh! How I dreaded the long walk home! I thought about the eggs that had to be gathered before they froze, the chickens that needed feed and fresh water, the corn cobs to be carried into the kitchen for fuel to keep the kitchen warm, and for cooking. Also, Bessie, my cow had to be milked, and those hungry calves had to be fed. I dreaded to leave the warm cheerful fire and lingered even longer. Beulah encouraged me as she helped me bundle up in my coat, overshoes, mittens, and scarves. Then Frank said, "Can I take you home with the wagon and team?"

His kind caring words made me tremble inside with fear. I was so afraid of Mama. I often wonder if that fear showed. I could hear Mama's demand—**never, never** accept a ride; you are to walk home **understand**! I did not want to disobey her, then be scolded or have her make fun of me, or to be told that I'd "sinned against God" because I had disobeyed her. I wanted to be loved—not pushed away. I knew I dared not accept his kindness.

I quickly replied, "I have to walk." I left as quickly as I could and crunched the frosty snow homeward bound. I feared what would happen when I arrived home when I realized that it was almost dark. I tried to hurry but I was so bundled up that it was very difficult to rush facing that icy gale and the deep snow.

I arrived home very cold but safe. I was fearful of punishment because of my disobedience. I arrived just as Mama came into the house from doing her chores. She angrily asked, "Why are you so late? It was so cold that I had to gather the eggs before they froze. Now hurry up and git into your chores clothes and git your chores done. It is dark, now you'll have to take this lantern so you can see. Now hurry! What was wrong that you are so late?" Without an answer, I did as I was told.

I hated to carry that smelly, old, kerosene lantern. I needed to be very careful where I set it. In the milk barn I could hang the lantern on a nail on the wall as I needed both hands to milk Bessie. I was worried because I knew if the lantern would fall over; it could cause a fire. The fire would burn everything quickly and I could even be burned. If that happened it would be my fault. We could be homeless. I felt so badly for my disobedience. I quickly left the house to do my chores out in the cold darkness.

I finished my chores and came into the kitchen just as Mama finished cooking supper. We sat down to a hot delicious meal of fresh, homemade bread, sour cream (which we used as butter), fried potatoes and gravy, home-canned green beans, and browned fat meat for me. My dad had fried ham. Mama said the lean meat was for the men. I had to eat the fat meat, as it would be a "sin to throw away the riches God gave us." I was not allowed to eat gravy on my potatoes, as that would be mixing two different starches.

* * *

Years later, after I received my driver's license, I would occasionally stop at the Graham home, to visit with these dear neighbors. During one visit Frank surprised me with "Do you remember a very cold, snowy, windy day when you were little, you stopped here to warm up on your way home from school?" I shyly nodded afraid the guilt of my disobedience might still show on my face. He continued, "I offered to take you home with the team and wagon but you insisted on walking."

My quick reply was, "Yes, I remember that night." I tried to hide the embarrassment I felt because of my disobedience and his surprise question. Yet in the back of my mind I was pleased he had remembered that bitter cold, snowy night those many years before as he had verified that that night had not been something in my imagination but facts. I still regret I never told him why I could not accept his kind and caring offer. But somehow I felt he knew because all the neighbors knew of the unrealistic expectations set for me. He continued, "Did you know I followed you with the team and wagon? I had to know you had made it home safely?"

"No," I replied. As I think of the past and that night in particular, I realize God had sent a guardian angel to watch over me before I knew of His all caring love. Now I say: "I am so blessed!" Those thoughts bring tears to my eyes just thinking of God's ever encompassing love. "**Thank you, God for your ever caring love.**"

DOLLY

What a surprise! Christmas time excited me when the box from Grandpa Grams arrived. In it were tangerines which we called "oranges", hard candy, English walnuts (that I never liked), lovely used wool garments, and a small new gift for me. This year I received a lovely doll. The doll was my special gift, my first dolly. She had lovely long golden curls, eyes that opened and closed and movable arms and legs. Her dress was a lovely pink floral print with white lace trim, white anklets and black patent leather shoes. I named her "Dolly."

When I returned to school after Christmas vacation, the other girls had brought their new dolls to show, and play with. I had not taken Dolly to school and the other girls would neither allow me to see or play with them, or their dolls. I was sad and lonely; I wanted my dolly. My thoughts turned to my dolly home all alone in the cold front room, while I was sat all alone at school. How I wanted to have my dolly, too. As soon as I arrived home, I asked, "Mama, can I take my doll to school tomorrow? The other girls brought their new dolls to school today to play with, but they would not let me play with their dolls."

"No, you're not takin' your doll to school!" she retorted in a demanding tone. I was hurt; I thought, "Do you understand how I felt, or do you care?" I would be the only girl without a doll. Sadly, I changed into my chore clothes and started doing my chores. I kept wondering how I could take my doll to school without Mama's knowledge. I wanted to be accepted by the other girls, and I felt I was not accepted because I had no new doll like the other girls had. Yet I was dressed differently, which included braided long hair, long brown cotton stockings and a different style dress. Finally, I had an idea.

The next morning I did my chores as usual. I had my usual breakfast a half-cup of cooked tomatoes. My lunch was ready; I shrugged into my coat, then went into my bedroom, and quickly tucked Dolly next to me under my coat. I tried to act normal, but evidently I must have done something that looked suspicious to Mama. I had a fun day with Dolly.

That evening as I was walked in the driveway towards the yard gate, inside the yard fence, I saw a figure the size of my dad with angry eyes glaring at me –"Eagle eyes"—he called it. I was too frightened to take a second look to see if the figure had horns and a twitching tail. "Oops"! I thought and trembled. "Mama checked and knows what I did;" she told dad. "Now I'm in real trouble!" My heart pounded as I walked into the house. I was so frightened but I had to hide my fear. I knew dad had a quick temper. The way he looked at me that moment, I was afraid he'd beat me to a pulp or tear me to pieces. I wanted to run away.

He followed me into the house and grabbed his razor strop. It was two strips of soft leather about two inches wide and twenty inches long that he used to put the fine edge on his straight razor before his weekly shave. He was ready to hit me. I do not recall that he did. Mama stopped him as her thoughts flashed back to her childhood, when she lived with her Uncle Jacob after her mother's death. At the age of three and half, Uncle Jacob made her herd cattle walking on the open range; if she displeased him, he'd horse whip her. From that day on I was not allowed to call my dad "Dad." Mama said, "You call him "E.B." which were his initials.

Mama worried for weeks about that razor strop. Finally, during the summer, I hid the strop while Mama was taking her afternoon nap. No comments were made about the missing razor strop.

I went into my bedroom. How sad I felt when I took Dolly from under my coat and saw that one of her arms was missing! I could have cried right then but did not dare. I had no idea what happened to the arm or when it came off. It was tightly attached so could not have just fallen off. I suspected that Birdena was the culprit, as she always seemed to be against me.

* * *

I was reminded of an incident with Birdena the year before. My first year in school when I had been so frightened when school started; I could not talk for six weeks. When I did start talking, I was promoted to grade two. Birdena and I were no longer in the same class.

For Christmas that year, Grandpa's special gift had been a pencil box with two pretty yellow pencils. The other children had the plain brown penny pencils. When I took one of my yellow pencils to school, with Mama's permission, Birdena was envious. She was determined to have my yellow pencil. Was it the only yellow pencil in the school? I didn't know. But at noon I saw Birdena playing with my yellow pencil outside in the school yard. She had taken **my** pencil from inside my desk. I was angry and said, "Birdena, that pencil is mine! Give it to me!"

"No! This is my pencil!" she angrily retorted, as she pulled her hand back against her chest tightly gripping my pencil.

"No, it's mine; you took it from my desk. Give me my pencil; my Grandpa sent that to me from California." I replied, as I reached for my pencil. She quickly snapped it into two pieces then flung the two pieces on the ground before she punched me in the nose with a hard blow of her fist. I cried and cried. My nose hurt; blood dripped on my dress and my yellow pencil was broken. I wondered – could she have done something to my Dolly's arm? Now my beautiful dolly had only one arm; my only other toy was an old teddy left by my brothers. Teddy was best described by the play poem (author unknown):

33

Fuzzy Wuzzy was a bear,
A bear was Fuzzy Wuzzy
When Fuzzy Wuzzy lost his hair
He wasn't Fuzzy, was he?

I was so thankful that Birdena did not accompany Miss Stamn to school the next year.

JULY FOURTH

July fourth was approaching. Mama decided that we would have our own firework display, as we never attended any of the firework displays at Benkelman. She and I chose several different kinds of firework explosives: long thin ones, large ones, short squatty ones and the wee "fire crackers."

After dark on July 4th, I built a mound of sand in our driveway to keep a long thin tube upright and Mama lighted it. I was so anxious to see what that long colorful tube contained. Not a "bang" but bright fire balls emerged with a loud "boom" as they sored high up into the sky; bright, colorful sparks rained down. A second ball came just seconds later, another "boom" and more beautiful sparks.

When we began lighting the fireworks, we never thought about the horses outside in the corral near the barn. They were normally tied inside the barn but that night it was cooler outside. The "booms" from the fireworks frightened the horses. They raced around and around the four-wire, barbed wire, corral fence with each loud boom. I was so terrified and afraid that they would try to go over or through the barbed wire fence that the fun of the fireworks was nixed. I knew I would never hear the last of it from my dad if the horses became injured. "Craziness" he'd call it.

A day or two later I tried to light a few of the firecrackers nearer the house. The first one I lighted exploded in my hand before I could toss it away. I had powder burns on my hand and arm and could not hear with my left ear for several weeks. I was just seven years old. We never repeated this celebration.

* * *

A fondly recalled July 4th celebration was quieter and very enjoyable. My brothers were still home. I was very young. We made homemade ice cream, a rare treat. Alvin and Lyle retrieved ice blocks from our icehouse back of the chicken house. The ice had been cut with a saw from the stock water tank during the previous winter and stored in the icehouse packed in layers of hay. This ice was crushed then layered with rock salt around the ice cream container in the wooden freezer bucket. My brothers turned the crank on the ice cream freezer until it was hard to turn. This meant the ice cream was ready to be served. That was the last year we had ice in the icehouse.

This was an extra special occasion as we shared it with Uncle Andy, Aunt Grace, and their children, Harry, Eva and Edna. What a wonderful treat to share and a wonderful way to celebrate our nation's birthday!

HAIL

The dark clouds rolled as the thunder grew louder and lightning flashed. The gale-like wind roared but I was not afraid. I ran here and there and picked up the just fallen large marble-sized hail stones wiped them on my dress before I popped the cold, icy chunks into my mouth. What a cooling treat after an extremely hot day! Mama yelled, "Com' back." as I continued further and further from the house.

Finally, Mama became impatient, she screamed, "Com' in 'fore you git hurt." A few seconds later, a very loud crash of thunder was followed by blinding flashes of lightning. I jumped with fright and dashed towards the house. I had just closed the door when the wind, rain, and hail blasted the house. The gale-like wind drove the hail-filled rain through window screens with such force it caused one glass pane to crack. Crack went another window pane! "Quick," Mama commanded, "Git the potato masher and big spoons, and help me push the screens away from the glass." She was standing at the west bedroom window where the glass had broken, and held the screen away from the glass with her hand.

I found the requested items quickly then took my place at the south window. She remained at the west window of the bedroom. The storm was brief. We were so thankful for the rain and that only two small window panes had been broken. The hail ruined all our crops.

A HORSE AND A SAND BUR

Horses have been man's beasts of burden for years. They have been used to help people hunt for food, to fight wars, for entertainment, and for travel.

When I attended grade school in western Nebraska in the 1930's, horses were used as "school buses." Children from three families at my school rode a horse to school. A small horse barn was provided for the animals' comfort and protection from the weather. Hay was provided but no water as we did not have a well at school.

The Ferguson family lived over three miles from school. The state law stated that children living more than three miles from school would be paid transportation fees based on the child's daily attendance. The Ferguson children were the only ones to qualify.

Willis and Leitha rode on a large, gentle, brown work horse. A work horse was trained to wear leather harness and pull wagons or farm equipment. They were not light-footed animals or fast like riding horses. Most of the children rode bare back, without a saddle.

After school, one cold, late October day, I was invited to ride with Willis and Leitha as they were going to my house to collect their transportation check. My dad, the school treasurer for District #37, wrote the checks.

The weather had been cold, crisp, and dry for days; perfect harvest weather. It was, also, perfect weather for the ripe, pesky, sand bur, weed seeds to be distributed. These weeds had grown abundantly and the vines were generously loaded. The small, round, ball-like seeds were covered with short spines, which would catch on anything that touched it.

I was able to climb up on that tall brown horse when I stood on the frame of the teeter-totter. Willis handled the reins, Leitha sat behind him; and I was behind Leitha. I felt so privileged to be riding a horse, my first horseback ride. The chilly weather required mittens. I held my lunch pail in my right hand then noticed a sand bur on my left hand mitten. I could not take my mitten off to pick the bur off. I choose the only choice left—my teeth. I am not sure if the plodding of the horse, or what caused me to draw in my breath. The bur that I held lightly between my teeth was drawn in with my breath and was down my throat in an instant. I coughed and cried, and cried and coughed, but that bur was secure.

When we arrived at my home, I was still crying. Going to the doctor was not an option, Mama did not believe in medical doctors. She did not drive anyway, so there was no way to get me to the doctor 25 miles away.

After the Fergusons had left for their home, Mama again explained that there would be no use going to the doctor regardless how much my throat hurt. And hurt it did! She gave me a raw egg white to swallow. She recalled a recent article in our weekly paper about a child who had swallowed a sand bur. That child had been rushed to the doctor. An X-ray had not shown where the sand bur was located. "We do not have money to throw away like that," she continued.

That bur remained—wherever it had lodged until June of the next year. A sharp tickle in my throat caused me to begin a hard coughing spell. Soon that bur emerged, crisp, and surrounded with phlegm and a touch of blood.

THE DUST STORM

As the dark, reddish-colored sun peeked over the dusty haze of the horizon, everyone wondered what mystery the day would bring. When I looked toward the far northwest horizon, a small dark cloud-like image appeared with the slightest rolling movement. It looked like a far away, fuzzy, grounded thunderhead. There was a very eerie mysterious feeling without a breeze stirring, yet some motion surrounded us. Dust storms were not unfamiliar on the Great Plains in the 1930's. Something was different this day; everyone was uneasy and watched the sky.

Our usual morning chores were quickly done. When I was nearly ready for school, E.B. said, "I'll take you to school today as I will be goin' right past the school. The Lutz are shellin' corn. I'm to help. I'll be ready as soon as I get my scoop shovel." I was really surprised, as I always had to walk to school.

My teacher and other students stopped to gaze at the visible haze as it hovered in the sky and covered the sun before we went inside the school. A faint odor of dust was in the air. As we looked towards the northwest horizon, that dark image had grown larger. Now it looked like a big, black, distant cloud; a dust storm was coming. The anxious feelings about the day's weather increased. The wind blew stronger with a faint distant roar. The dust cloud's roll was visible as we entered the schoolhouse.

Recess came an hour and half later. Now the sky was very dark. The dust cloud surrounded us. The wind had gained in strength, and the whirling roar was closer. As the rolling, reddish, blackish dust cloud approached it sucked up the sand of our own soil. Soon more dry dust filled the air. We did not play but stood outside transfixed by the dust-filled air that surrounded us. We were anxious and cautious. There was no escape.

Around 11 a.m., during our arithmetic classes, parents began to arrive to take their children home. The children who had ridden a horse were told to turn the horse loose as it would find its way home. With heavy hearts, the children turned their horses loose, picked up the bridles, and went home with their parents.

Now the sky was very black and dark, the sun had disappeared. The wind was quite strong. School was dismissed as it was too dark in the classroom to see. As I was prepared to walk home, E.B. stopped enroute and picked me up.

Again, I was so surprised as he had never done that before. I asked him about the corn shelling. He said they had quit as they felt everyone needed get to their own homes because of the storm.

Almost immediately, the dust became so thick in the air that E.B. could barely see the road but he did keep the car, a 1933 Ford V-8 sedan, in the wheel track road. The headlights were on but the lights showed nothing except the black dust that swirled all around us. As he drove up our lane, he suddenly stopped the car, turned off the motor, and jumped out. He ran to the front of the car. "Why did you stop here?" I asked.

"I think I saw somethin' move in front of the car," he replied. Sure enough there was something. Lyle had come home and Mama had asked him to go after me with the team and wagon. She was afraid I would lose my way in the swirling darkness. The horses had become disoriented. They refused to go forward and were headed towards the house not the road. Lyle was afraid to get out of the wagon to lead them back to the barn. E.B. grabbed the bridles and led them to the barn, while Lyle stayed in the wagon holding the reins. When they were near the barn, they unhitched the horses from the wagon, led them inside, tied them in their stalls, and then removed the harnesses.

Quickly, I got out of the car and started to walk slowly toward the house. Occasionally, I could see something that I recognized as the dust-filled air swirled around me. I noticed something white on the ground near my feet. I bend over to touch it and discovered a confused chicken squatted down on the ground to keep its feathers from being turned backward, and to keep the wind from blowing it away. I picked it up and started to the chicken house. I had found several more chickens. I took all to their place of safety – the chicken house.

When we got inside the house, it was so dark that the lamp had to be lit so we could see. It was just after noon. The wind blew very hard and added more Nebraska soil to the dust that had been picked up in other states. By evening the wind calmed, but the air was so saturated with dust that it was still difficult to breathe. A moist rag held in front of the nose helped prevent breathing in the dust. I do not recall if we tried to eat a noon meal.

When evening chore time came, many of the cows were still out in the pasture where they had been when the dust storm had hit. The cattle were so frightened; they constantly bawled in the dusty darkness to reassure each other of their presence. We cared for the animals that had come to the corral. The next morning we had to immediately milk the cows that had remained out in the pasture all night.

The next day the sun rose bright and shiny in the clear blue sky. The dust-covered world was calm with drifts of dust everywhere. In the house, everything was dust covered. Touching anything left a gritty feel on the hands. Even inside the cabinets, the shelves and dishes were dust covered. Freshly prepared food had a dusty, gritty taste for several days. The odor of dust was everywhere. Windows sealed with tape didn't keep out the dust. This storm, one of our worst storms, created darkness that could not be penetrated with any type of light.

I have been asked to describe a dust storm, but words cannot adequately describe the darkness, the swirling dust, and the uncertainty of the atmospheric conditions. Can you imagine darkness so absorbing, and intense that you could not see your hand held just in front of your face during midday? The feelings of being in dry, dusty darkness at noonday, or to become lost and disoriented in your own back yard are impossible to document.

* * *

A common joke was often repeated: A man from the East had come to Nebraska and wanted to buy a farm. He visited with the local diners in a small café. A farmer mentioned he had a farm for sale. The man from the East became very interested and asked, "Could we go and take a look at your farm? I want to purchase some real estate here."

The farmer held his coffee cup, while he looked out the window watching a dark, gray cloud. He could see a dark, dust cloud rolling on the distance horizon. Finally, he drawled, "Just be patient and wait, it will soon be comin' past!"

GRASSHOPPERS

Grasshopper swarms came in the early 1930's, a result of the drought, and soil robbing, dust storms. The dust storms were the result of very little rainfall and farmers trying to cultivate very sandy soil. The grasshoppers came in hordes, and were everywhere. They would eat anything made of a plant product, which included pitchfork, and spade handles, and even fence posts were chewed on after soft edible plants, corn, hay, any other crops, and the more tender parts of the trees had been being depleted.

To assist the desperate farmers in their battle to survive, the government provided free poison "mash." This product was sawdust flavored with banana oil and a very poisonous insecticide. The aroma was deliciously alluring and naturally attracted the insects. It was to be scattered in the weeds and grass along the fence rows, at the end of corn, and cane (a hay crop) rows, and any other places where farm animals would not be feeding.

My dad loaded the big bags of the mash into a wagon. Then Mama and I went to the fields. The team walked slowly to pull the wagon along the selected areas; both of us would scatter the mash bare-handed from the wagon among the weeds. As the mash was thrown into the weeds, the grasshoppers would swarm up into the air creating "a roar like a motor." I had helped Mama several times. The next thing I knew was that my right hand so swollen that I could not close it. I couldn't milk my cows.

I was really scolded by E.B. because I could not do my share of the milking. My hand wasn't painful, but it was too swollen to close. It was nearly two weeks before I could close it.

* * *

E.B.'s response to my swollen hand reminded me of one school morning when I got up sick. Mama allowed me to stay in bed while she went to milk; she said she would milk my cows. When she returned she had a black eye, and her face was swollen. "What happened?" I anxiously inquired.

"Oh, Ellis got on his 'high horse' this morning and threw his milk stool at me." she angrily replied. That was the first time I had actually seen Mama with bruises from E.B. hitting her. She had often talked about his cruelty but this was the first visible result.

I thought to myself, Mama must have forgotten what she had been teaching me. **Be quiet, don't rock the boat**. I wondered—did she speak up about something?

BABY RABBITS

As my dad planted the corn, he would sometimes plow out baby rabbits hidden within their nests. We were told that if the nest was disturbed, or destroyed, the mother rabbit would not return. I raised seven rabbits one summer: six jack rabbits and a cottontail. Most of them were so tiny when I first started to care for them that I fed them milk a drop at a time with a medicine dropper. When they were old enough, they were kept outside in a wire poultry-netting fence with the netting on top to protect them from hawks, the dog, or cat. I provided them with tender grass, clover, soda crackers for salt, and other fresh foods. They did very well.

At night I brought them all into the house to the blocked off a portion of the floor in front of the open front room door in Mama's and my bedroom. I wanted to keep them safe. The fresh clover and tender grass was stuffed into small flat jars of water, and fresh soda crackers were laid on the floor. Our sleep was often interrupted. Rabbits are nocturnal animals which are very active at night.

I provided protection from predators: hawks, coyotes, dog, or cat. But never once thought of one predator. We were eating our noon meal, when we heard boisterous' chattering ruckus outside from the chickens that were always in the yard. Immediately, I dashed to the door and was saddened and angry. I saw that a bull snake had crawled through the one-inch netting fence and was trying to swallow a one-fourth grown jack rabbit, one of my rabbits.

All the rabbits were frightened but the little cottontail was so terrified that it found a hole in the fence that I did not know existed. It quickly scampered away. After the snake was disposed of, I opened the pen and let the rest go. They were all old enough now to take care of themselves.

SNAKES

There were a lot of non-poisonous snakes around our barnyard. They were welcomed as they feasted on the rats and mice which were abundant on our farm. They slithered down into the rodent's dens to feast on the baby rodents. I was not afraid of the bull snakes, a non-poisonous snake. It was not unusual to see me carry a bull snake at arms' length around the yard. I held it by the tip of its tail with its head nearly touching the ground.

* * *

One day I found a bull snake in trouble. I had gone out to the horse barn to check for eggs in the horse feed boxes. As I approached the open barn door, I saw the tail half of a snake lying on the ground out from a knothole in the flat, wooden, barn siding with a large, round lump within its body. I puzzled about the strange appearance until I stepped into the barn. I saw head half of the snake with a large, round lump in its body. I mused softly, "Poor thing, you were selfish; now you have a problem. You can't go anywhere until you digest the eggs you swallowed. You greedy ol' snake; you can stay there until you digest your 'pot-o'-gold'!"

Snakes love eggs because they are so easy to swallow whole as a snake does with all of its food. I wasn't afraid of a bull snake but I wanted to see it first. When I gathered eggs and reached in a nest that was just above my eyesight, I always feared I'd touch the cold, scaly body of a snake. If I touched a snake, cold shivers would race down my spine. There would be no eggs after the snake feasted. The snake rested in the nest for the eggs to digest before it moved on for new explorations.

*   *   *

I was very afraid of being bitten by a poisonous diamond-back rattlesnake. These snakes had a tail with dry scales that grew in length each time the snake shed its skin. The snake would vibrate its tail as it prepared to strike. Rattlesnakes are dark gray in color with a black diamond designs on its back. I had heard it said a rattlesnake is always a gentleman. Meaning, it will not strike without rattling its tail as a warning. Don't believe it. Any snake—poisonous, or non-poisonous, or rattlesnake will strike if it feels it is threatened. Best advice: beware of all snakes!

CHICK

(Featured in Heroic Pets, August 30, 1998 in The Sunday Herald Times)

The summer I was ten, we had a frail white leghorn chick that needed a lot of TLC. I chose that job. "Chick" was an appropriate name for the little white chick as it was always saying "chick, chick" as it pecked away at the special morsels that I provided.

June mornings in western Nebraska were usually quite cool. The sun was arched toward the sky's summit with hot rays of the sun warming the cool earth. Chick had begged for its special treats. I went out onto the back porch. With my back to the hot sun, I was busy tugging on the lid of tall tin can on the porch to get Chick's favorite grains.

Suddenly Chick's begging turned into a flurry of fearful chatterings. The usual chattering sounds made by chickens when they are fearful of something on the ground, usually a snake. I ignored Chick's chatterings as my thoughts were on getting the lid removed from the can.

Inside the house Mama had heard the Chick's sounds of fear, and stepped to the back screen door to investigate the reason. "Freeze!" she demanded, "Don't move, and stay right where you are!" Then she disappeared; I was puzzled, but I did not move.

In a flash, she came around the house with a garden hoe. She immediately struck and killed the diamond-back rattlesnake that had silently crawled up, and coiled just behind my bare feet to warm itself in the hot morning sun. Its eight-rattle tail was very visible extended above its coiled body.

"Thank you, Chick!" I silently thought. "Today you have been my guardian angel!" I gave Chick an extra handful of her favorite grains.

TOMMY

Cats are necessary on a farm as they can live on the mice and rats that always invade the farm to feast on the grain provided for the cows, hogs, horses, and chickens. We had a hard time to keep a cat, as the coyotes killed them. But we had one cat that survived with his "nine lives" for several years. He had a white nose and soft white underside with a slick, shiny, black coat. Somehow, he had escaped capture by the coyotes.—Tommy was a smart cat.

It was my job to feed Tommy. To show his appreciation for the milk and petting, Tommy brought me gifts of his favorite foods – mice, moles, and kangaroo rats. When he brought one of his "treats," he would lay it on the back porch near the kitchen door. Then he loudly "meowed" while he proudly twitched his tail, waiting for me to come and claim his "gift." I always awarded him with "nice kitty, nice kitty" as I stroked his shiny, black back, and rubbed his ears. He would curl his body around my ankles while his tail twirled and twisted in time to his loudest purr. I always accepted his gift—Tommy was a happy cat.

One summer morning when I came out on the porch before Tommy had called me, I saw he had a struggling half-grown cottontail bunny. I felt resentful, as the cottontails were special. They were smaller than the jackrabbits and stayed near the farm buildings as protection from the coyotes. As I bent over Tommy, I gently said, "No, Tommy you are not to catch the bunnies." I petted his head and talked gently to him, and hoped to get him to open his mouth and release his strangling grip on the struggling bunny.

Finally, he released his jaws just a wee bit as he lifted his head for more of the beloved petting. That allowed the bunny to fall from his mouth, flatten out on the ground, and in a split second, it scampered away out of the yard. I will never forget the deep look of defeat, and mistrust in Tommy's downcast, green eyes as he slinked away toward the barn dragging his long, black tail. If he could have spoken I am sure he would have said, "I trusted you and now look what you have done with my nice, warm, fresh treat! You betrayed me!"

He felt I did not appreciate his efforts and sacrifices when I tricked him to let his most prized meal escape. I felt badly as I had no intentions to insult faithful Tommy. Sadly he never trusted me with another "treat" Tommy was a –smart cat but now he was –a sad, sad cat!

FOOD

Bread

What a wonderful aroma on bread baking day! My mouth watered when I saw the loaves of fresh, golden, brown bread! I was tempted to reach for a bread knife and slice off a piece, but I did not dare. No piecing between meals.

Mama always kept a walnut-sized piece of raw bread dough in the flour pan in the cabinet. This ball of unbaked dough dried and provided the needed yeast for a new batch of bread. We had dried yeast years before it was available in grocery stores.

The evening before Mama planned to bake bread, she would take the little ball of dry dough and put it into a quart canning jar with the cooled liquid that she had drained from the boiled, supper potatoes. She added a little flour, sugar and salt and set the jar near the stove to keep it warm to help the yeast grow. The next morning the mixture would be separated into three layers: the flour mixture was above the semi-clear liquid in the center with some flour mixture at the bottom of the jar. It fascinated me to watch the yeast action. Every few minutes the mixture on the bottom would rise and then explode like miniature volcanoes.

The active yeast was ready to be combined with more flour, salt, and lard. Mama stirred it with a wooden spoon until it became a stiff dough. With freshly washed hands, she placed a large handful of flour on the breadboard, worked the flour into the dough until it was stiff, and then she kneaded it until it was smooth and shiny, and not longer clung to her hands. Then she folded the dough into a large, round loaf and placed it into the clean, greased dishpan, and covered with a clean, damp dishtowel to rise. The pan was set near the heat to help it rise quickly, which would take about an hour to double in size. She kneaded it down again and let it rise a second time before she formed it into loaves. These loaves were placed in well, greased loaf pans and allowed to rise again.

When the loaves were nearly double in size, Mama would build a hot fire to heat the oven. The loaf pans were set in the hot oven. Without a built-in heat thermometer in the door, the oven temperature was guess work. Every now and then she would open the oven door and take a quick peek. The loaves were done when the top was golden brown. She'd remove them from the oven and set them to cool before storing in the breadbox drawer of the Hoosier-made kitchen cabinet.

The leftover dough from the loaves would be rolled out with a handless, wooden, rolling pin until about one-half inch thick, then spread with butter, and topped with cinnamon and sugar. It was rolled into a long roll, sliced with a butcher knife into two-inch segments, and placed into a greased, shallow, aluminum, baking pan and allowed to rise until double. After the loaves of bread were baked, the cinnamon rolls were baked. I loved homemade bread but the taste of the oven-fresh cinnamon rolls were out of this world.

Butter

While the bread was baking, cream would be churned into butter. I would stand beside the three-gallon crockery churn to pull and push the dasher in the churn to stir the cream. We used sour cream, as it would separate into fat globs and buttermilk more quickly than sweet cream.

After the cream solids formed fat globs, Mama removed it from the churn and put it into a bowl. Then she poured cool water over it and kneaded it until all of the milk was removed from the fat globs and the water was clear. The butter was salted lightly. If company was expected, we pressed the fresh butter into a square butter mold with a pineapple design in the bottom. When the butter had set, the butter mold was turned upside down on a plate; the butter would fall on the plate with a nice designed top. It was ready to be spread on some fresh bread. Yum! Yum!

Cheese

We made our own cottage cheese using skimmed, sour milk. Sometimes we used Rennet, which we purchased at the grocery store, to help the milk curds collect into clumps quickly. The milk with, or without the Rennet would be heated to just below boiling then removed from the heat. Stirring helped the curds separate from the liquid. After the mixture had cooled, it would be poured into a clean sugar sack, which was a white light-weight cloth bag. The liquid or whey was pressed out as much as possible without pressing the curds out through the cloth. The sack was hung to drip.

After several hours, the curds were ready to be removed from the sack and placed into a bowl and lightly salted. Cream could be added for a creamy-tasting cottage cheese. It took a large quantity of milk to make a small batch of cottage cheese as milk is about 80 percent liquid. Today this cheese would be called "Farmer's Cheese."

Meat

We butchered one hog for meat during a cold day of winter. The hams, shoulders, and sides were all cured with smoked salt and packed in a wooden barrel set north of the house. The trimmings from the large meaty pieces were ground into sausage, seasoned with salt, pepper, and sage, and then fried. While hot the sausage patties were packed in syrup buckets then covered with fresh, hot lard. This sausage kept until late in the spring. The fat portion of the meat was rendered for lard and cracklings. The fresh lard was stored in syrup buckets and kept on the cool floor in the water room under the water trough, or stored in the cool fruit cellar.

The hog's head was not wasted. First the ears were cut from the head, singed and scrubbed with a brush and soap, rinsed then tossed into a large pot. The teeth in the jaw bones were scrubbed with a brush and soap and rinsed, and added to the pot with the ears.

Finally the skull was sawed open; the brains were removed, and these bones were toss into the pot. Other available meat scraps were added to the pot. The contents of the pot were cooked until the meat fell from the bones. The bones were removed and given to the dog. The cooked meat was chilled and served as "headcheese." The brains were delicious either scrambled with eggs, or cooked in water with a little vinegar (my favorite dish.). Only the squeal and the eyes were discarded.

On butchering day I carried water to rinse the uncut carcass, carried the cut pieces of meat into the house, and helped make the headcheese, and grind the sausage. Other tasks were often given to me, too.

* * *

Fat hens were baked. Young roosters were culled from the flock of pullets and fried. Around the age of eight, I was the taught to take a chicken, hold both legs and wings in my left hand and then the grasp the axe with my right hand and chop off the chicken's head as it lay on a large, wooden block. After it bled about 10 minutes, I would dunk the chicken into a bucket of near boiling water for a few seconds and start plucking (removing) the feathers. I even learned to cut up the chicken, and prepare it to fry or bake.

* * *

Young jack rabbits were plentiful. When I was around ten I was on my way home from school. As I walked through the cornfield, I noticed something black, round, and shiny about ten feet ahead of me in a clump of dry corn leaves. I approached cautiously. Sure enough a rabbit was crouched low trying to hide next to the corn stalks. I made a quick grab for the back of his neck, and caught the half-grown jackrabbit.

Quickly, I ran home with a tight grip on the rabbit and flew into the house to show Mama. "I caught this rabbit as it sat among corn stalks and leaves. Can we have it for supper? I'll dress it." I expounded as I caught my breath. We had fresh fried rabbit for supper that night. It was very tasty as there was no buck shot to pick out which made it even more palatable.

* * *

When I was 18, I took our 22-repeating single-shot Remington rifle and went rabbit hunting. I had not gone far into the pasture just north of the house, when I thought I saw something in the sagebrush clump about 20 feet ahead of me. I shot and could not believe it; the bullet hit a rabbit in the head. I returned the rifle to the bedroom rack and retired from rabbit hunting with a perfect record.

Vegetables and Fruits

I was the vegetable gardener starting at the age of eight. I grew green beans, tomatoes, leaf lettuce, turnips, cucumbers, beets, and more for eating fresh. All surplus vegetables were canned.

Mama used the cold pack canning method. She had heard that a little vinegar added to the top of a jar of the green beans would help the beans keep, using cold pack canning method. She usually purchased one or two bushels of green beans at the Thursday, farmer's produce market at the sale barn in Benkelman. I helped can 100 quarts or more of green beans and tomatoes each summer. We bought and canned tomatoes, peaches, concord grapes, and apples. Mama and I were busy canning foods all summer for the coming winter. We, also, made gallons of dill pickles, water melon pickles, jam, jellies, juice, and lots of kraut.

One summer when I was helping peel and remove the stones from peaches for canning, Mama brought water to the large pan I was working in and started to pour it into the pan. I stuck my hands into the water, thinking it was cold water. Instead it was boiling water. Both of my hands were scalded and I quit working on peaches. "Why did you stick your hands in that water?" Mama questioned.

I replied, "I thought you had cold water to rinse my sticky hands."

During the summer when I was especially hungry, I'd slip down into the fruit cellar and open a quart jar of grape juice and drink as much as I could. I'd put the lid on the jar and set the jar behind other jars. The next day I go down into the cellar and finished the juice, put the lid on the jar and set it back with the empty jars. More than once Mama expressed surprise that some of the empty jars were sticky on the outside when she washed them for canning. I remained mum. Once I ate a whole quart of grape jelly; I was so hungry.

It was usually my task to go down the cellar to get jars of canned food for a meal. One day I rushed down the stairway to get a jar of tomatoes. I quickly pulled back the curtain that protected the jars from light when the cellar door was opened. As I reached for a jar, but before I could pick it up, something jumped on my hand and zipped up my arm. What was a shock! I screamed! I am not sure who was more surprised me or that mouse. His feet had very sharp toes. My heart was racing 90 miles a minute as I flew up the stairs and into the house with the jar to tell Mama about the mouse.

Fresh corn on the cob was relished. We did not grow sweet corn but used the regular field corn when it was just past the milk stage of development. We dried corn for winter use. We picked the ears, removed husks and silks, and then cut the kernels from the cobs. I spread the cut kernels on two clean dish towels. The towels were carried outside and laid on a flat surface to dry. Two clean dish towels were laid over the cut corn to protect it from the insects. It would take more than a week in the hot summer sun before the cut-off kernels were dry and rattled like dry beans. Then it was safe to store in a syrup bucket. To prepare the dried corn to eat, it was soaked overnight then cooked slowly on the back of the kitchen range. It was delicious.

Another form of corn that I loved to eat and helped prepare many times was hominy. I found this recipe when I visited the museum in Champion, Nebraska.

Lye Hominy

For each quart of white or yellow corn, dissolve 2 tbsp of lye in one gallon of water. Use an enamel kettle. Add corn and boil for 30 minutes until hulls loosen. Rinse corn thoroughly. Several changes of hot water will be needed to remove the lye. Then cover with cold water, rub to remove hulls and black tips.

Let stand in cold water 2-3 hours. Change water 2 or 3 times. (I do this out on the lawn.) Drain, cover with hot water, add 1 teaspoon salt to 1 quart of water. Boil until tender and drain. Serve.

Contributor Ada Kelly

We grew beans for dry beans between rows of corn in the field nearest to the house. I disliked shelling these beans as the dry bean pods had a peculiar odor which remained on hands and clothes plus they were dusty. Squash and pumpkins were grown in the cornfield, also.

THISTLES

Weeds grow in any soil, even when grass or crops cannot survive. The summer I was nine, we had a bumper crop of tumbleweeds and Russian thistles. Both weeds, when dry were big, round, woody-ball shaped, branched structures. These "balls" when broken off at ground level by animals, or the wind could roll for miles stopped only by permanent plants, fences, or buildings. The weeds would form stacks several feet high and wide. These "balls," a neat design of nature, could scatter seeds everywhere the wind may take it. But when these weeds collected at the edge of a corn field, they had to be burned before the corn was planted.

The following summer during corn planting, E.B. asked me to accompany him to the east field to burn the weeds while he planted corn. He took the team of six horses that were needed to pull the lister, and drove to the field. A lister was a plow-planter with two sets of double plows combined with a corn planter between each of the double plow blades. The seed kernels were dropped as the earth was plowed and planted at the same time. Small disc rolled soil over the kernels.

A huge stack of these weeds had collected along the south side of the field near the pasture fence. Some were half buried by the sand, and dust storms of the previous winter, and others were caught on last year's corn stalks.

E.B. tied the horses to the pasture fence near the north side of the field. Then he came to help me pull the weeds back from the barbed wire fence onto the weed pile collected in the field. He returned to the horses and began planting corn.

There was very little wind; a safe day to burn the weeds. I threw a lighted match into the dry weeds. Immediately, I had a very quick, hot fire. My task was quickly completed. I was ready to go home by 10 o'clock. I had worn my usual summer dress, wide-brimmed, straw hat, and shoes. I do not recall if I drank any water from the water jug that set in the wagon before I started home.

The cool morning had developed into very hot day. Around 10:00 o'clock, I began the two-mile walk home across the pasture. I was accustomed to walking in the heat; as usual I was covered with sweat. But when I was near to the barn yard, I suddenly quit sweating, and my skin felt cold. My head and my eyes were swimmery. "Will I be able to make it?" I mumbled to myself. "I can't fall here. I may not be found. There may even be a rattlesnake nearby." More puzzling thoughts circulated in my mind but I kept walking; I knew I should not stop. Finally, I arrived at the barnyard and was soon in the house.

The coolness in the house felt great! I drank some cool water; but felt very tired and weak. I headed for the bedroom to lie down, but when I was beside the bed that my brothers formerly slept in, every thing went black before my eyes. I fell on the bed and went to "sleep."

Sometime later when I awakened, I felt fine and my eyes and head were ok. I believe that the hot sun on my walk home had caused me to pass out. Mama never knew it. She was in the kitchen when I came home but just thought I had gone to the bedroom to take a nap.

*   *   *

That was the first time I passed out; the second time was the following summer. Mama kept a large flock of laying hens; she sold eggs. A very long chicken house was needed to house 100 hens. The walls of the original 50-foot section had been built and finished inside like a house with lathe and plaster. The wooden, shingled, shed roof was high at the south side with many windows to capture more sunshine for light and heat in the winter. The newer 50-foot section matched the original design except that it had unfinished walls. Both sections had a dirt floor.

Rats and mice moved in uninvited and feasted on the chicken feed and mash. The finished walls provided perfect nesting places for their families. Holes could easily be chewed in the plastered walls and tunnels dug into the dirt floor along the walls.

Frequently Mama tried to eradicate those critters. One year she tried cyanide gas, a white powder that we spooned into the rat holes with hopes the poisonous gas would kill the critters. She cautioned me not to breathe the gas but it was impossible not to get a whiff of it when the lid was off the can. I didn't have a mask over my nose as I spooned the powder into the rat and mice holes and plugged the openings with corn cobs as quickly as possible. This was a waste of time and money as those rodents were smart with many openings to their dens.

This particular summer, the summer I was 11, Mama decided to try to cover the holes in the walls with new plaster. I had to help. She mixed the dry, white, plaster powder with water to the correct consistency then showed me how to apply it with the metal trowel. With my bucket of wet plaster, I eagerly went to work using the trowel to slather it on the holes in the wall and smooth it. But after several foiled attempts, the wet plaster mixture would not stick on the dry plaster, I laid the trowel down. I took my bare right hand and began to smooth the creamy mixture onto the old plaster. All went well until I hit a sharp piece of rusty tin. An old tin can that had been flattened and nailed to the wall years before had a sharp protruding edge. I had not seen that sharp edge and slid my hand right over it. I did not feel the tin cut my finger but quickly saw the blood spurting. My right index finger was slit very deep from the tip to the first joint; it throbbed and felt numb.

I began to cry. Mama saw the blood drip. She rushed me to the house and poured clear, cold water over the cut, and found some clean white rags. She placed a quantity of flour in the center of the cloth. I laid my finger, cut-side down on the flour; then she wrapped the rag tightly around my finger. My finger throbbed. I did not feel well and headed for the bedroom to lie down. Again when I was beside my brothers' former bed, everything began to turn black before my eyes. My head felt strange as I started to lie down everything went black. I was out again.

Mama went back to the chicken house to use the plaster mixture before it hardened. I don't know how long I slept or was passed out before I awakened.

SEWING

I learned to sew using a foot-pedal-powered, belt-driven, black, Kenmore sewing machine when I was seven years old. I did not have a doll to make clothes for. I hemmed sugar sacks for dish towels. At that time sugar was sold in 50 and 100-pound cloth bags. The bags were made of light-weight white muslin-type fabric. I wanted to sew all of the time. I begged to make a quilt but Mama said that would not be profitable. I begged and begged to sew. Finally, she let me make some white flour sack underpants for myself. She helped me cut them out using her homemade pattern. These were knee length and worn in the summer under my dresses. They looked more like shorts. Wintertime underwear was "long johns" or long white underwear.

This unknown author said it well:

Depression Flour Sack Underwear
When I was just a maiden fair,
Mama made our underwear.
With many kids and Dad's poor pay,
We had no fancy lingerie.
Monograms and fancy stitches
Did not adorn our Sunday britches.
Pantywaists that stood the test
Had "Gold Medal" on my breast.
No lace or ruffles to enhance,
Just "Pride of Bloomington" on my pants.

One pair of panties beat them all
For it had a scene I still recall:
Harvesters were gleaning wheat
Right across my little seat.
Rougher than a grizzly bear
Was my flour sack underwear.
Plain, not fancy, and two feet wide
And tougher than a hippo's hide.
All through the Depression each Jill and Jack
Wore the sturdy garb of sack.
Waste not, want not, we soon learned
That a penny saved is a penny earned.
There were curtains and tea towels too,
And that is just to name a few,
But the best beyond compare
Was my flour sack underwear.

(From Poems collected by Mrs. Flance Shanley, Petoskey, MI.)

* * *

When I was 12, Mama received some medium blue cotton print fabric with a small rose floral design, a Christmas gift from Alvin. A large piece of fabric was left after Mama finished her dress, but not enough to make another dress. I thought some plain pink would be very nice to combine with this blue print. I begged and begged until Mama finally gave in and bought a yard of plain pink. We ordered a ten-cent, shirt waist, six-gored skirt dress pattern from the *Capper's Weekly* newspaper.

Now I had fabric for the dress that I had pictured in my mind using both the blue and pink colored fabrics. I made half of each bodice piece of the blue print and the other half plain pink. The sleeves and collar were half and half of each color. The gores in the skirt were alternated pink and blue. I made the buttonholes by hand. At last, I had my own color-block, designer dress. I was proud of my first dress. Mama was not impressed; she referred to it as "that old patched up thing." I loved it, but I was not allowed to wear it to school. My masterpiece but I could only wear it at home. How discouraging! My special work, perfect in my eyes, was just like trash according to Mama.

* * *

When I was around 13, Vera, Alvin's wife, gave me her old, black, fur-collared, wool coat. It was toasty warm, and fit nicely. I wore it to school. One day I accidentally caught it on a small nail that protruded from the school flag pole. The nail tore a large two-sided tear right in the center back at the shoulders. How terrible I felt! I was afraid that Mama would be so angry. What could I do? On the way home I thought, "I'll go immediately into the front room, our bedroom, and take my coat off, maybe Mama won't notice the tear." I succeeded with my plan. I did my evening chores and was mum about my coat.

Saturday morning chores, breakfast, and the laundry were done. Mama said she had some work to do in the chicken house. "Now," I thought, "I will get a needle with black thread from the sewing machine in the kitchen and go into the cold front room and try to mend my coat." I carefully wove the black thread, back and forth, pulling the broken fabric fibers underneath as best I could. I finished in record time.

I had worn my coat several days before Mama noticed the mended back. She asked what had happened; I told her. She surprised me when she said, "If you would have asked me, I would have fixed it." She didn't sound angry. I was afraid if she had mended it, there would have been a big, visible seam.

LAUNDRY

Laundry was done on a wash board when I was very young. Later it was simplified with a square-tub, gasoline-powered, Maytag washing machine. However, in the coldest weather, we could not use the washer. It was kept in the water room on the cement floor; the flexible, exhaust pipe had to be extended out of the back door. The open door let in too much icy cold air. That could cause things to freeze, as this room was never heated. Then the wash tub and wash board were used in the kitchen.

The washing machine had a power wringer, a wonderful invention. We could swivel the wringer to wring clothes from the washer into the first rinse tub, then from that rinse tub into the second rinse tub. Wringing overalls by hand was next to impossible, but even with the wringer, there were drawbacks with the buttons and buckles. Clothes had to be turned wrong side, out or the buttons could be popped off from the pressure of the firm wringer rollers. Fingers, a hand, or even an arm could easily be caught and pressed between the turning firm rubber rollers. My fingers, hands, and even my right arm went through the rollers unharmed more than once. Fortunately, my hair was braided and pinned around my head so it did not get caught.

The wet clothes were always hung outside on the clothes line to dry, winter and summer. On warm breezy days the clothes dried nice and fluffy; but on the coldest days of winter, the frozen garments were brought into the house hung behind the kitchen range to dry.

* * *

One summer day when I was around seven, I accidentally touched the hot exhaust pipe with my leg. Oh! How that burned! Mama immediately put a mixture of unsalted butter and sulphur on it then tied a white rag around my leg that made my leg burn even more.

I sobbed, as I ran around to the back of the chicken house followed by Brownie, our farm dog. He wagged his tail, came to me, and smelled my leg. The white rag had slipped to my ankle. Brownie quickly, but carefully licked off the butter-sulphur mixture. What a relief! The cool air felt great! When I returned to the house, Mama questioned, "What did you do with that bandage?"

I replied, "It fell off as I ran. Brownie came up to me, wagged his tail, smelled the butter-sulphur mixture, then carefully licked it off, and that made my leg feel much better."

* * *

We made our own laundry soap in the summer when the doors and windows could be open. Ingredients were lye, stale lard or cracklings, and water. The mixture was boiled until thick like honey, and then poured into a flat corrugated cardboard box to cure. The curing would take six to eight weeks. I always helped with the soap making but detested the task. The lye-grease mixture always left such an unpleasant greasy-lye odor that lingered in the house for days.

* * *

Our irons (flat irons) had removable handles and were heated on the kitchen range. They had to be very hot to iron damp starched garments without leaving brown streaks. One day I saw brown streaks on the front of my white school blouse. I complained. Mama said, "Ok, from now on you can do all the washin' and ironin.'" I was around 10 or 11 and from that day on every Saturday my job was doing the laundry. Yes, I even washed the clothes in the coldest winter using the wash board in the wash tub in the kitchen. When we washed in the kitchen we had to carry the wash water outside.

* * *

I was around 13 when Mama purchased a blue enamel and chrome gas iron; also, an ironing board with fold-up legs, and built-on sleeve board. What a great improvement from the irons we heated on the stove! I would fill the cup-sized tank on the iron with white gas, and pumped air into the tank with a tiny pump. Then I carefully lighted it. In a few minutes the iron was hot and ready to begin ironing. There was one temperature – hot. One drawback with this iron was the need to have plenty of ventilation because of the fumes from the burning gas. Ironing was fun, as the brown streaks, were a thing of the past.

COUSIN DOLLY

Mama's oldest sister, Aunt May, lived on a farm near Yorkton, Saskatchewan, Canada. She had a large family of twelve children. Her youngest child, Dolly, was four years younger than I. Aunt May and Dolly visited in Nebraska in 1938. They stayed most of the time with Uncle Andy, Aunt May's and Mama's brother. He had a large house with several bedrooms, while we had a small house with only one bedroom. They visited several times at our home during the year that they remained in Nebraska.

One time when they visited, school was in session. Dolly attended school with me. It was wonderful to have her walk to school with me and to play with during recess. My teacher asked her to sign the guest register book as all school visitors were asked to do. Dolly had three middle names; so her name took up the whole line. I was so proud of her. As an adult she dropped the name "Dolly," a shortened version of Dianne.

My school was very different than Dolly's Canadian school. Her farm home was two and a half miles from school. During the frigid Canadian winters when the temperature was 50 degrees below zero, it was too far to walk. During the school year her mother rented an apartment near the Yorkton School. Dolly and her siblings attended the city school. French was a required subject in the Canadian Schools.

Dolly liked our farm dog, Tippy. Mama had taught Tippy several tricks: roll over, sit up, beg, climb a ladder, and shake hands. Dolly enjoyed seeing Tippy perform her tricks.

Aunt Susan, another of Aunt May's and Mama's sisters, visited, also. She lived on a cattle ranch in western Montana. It was so nice to see my two aunties and one of my cousins all of whom lived so far from Nebraska.

In 1986 Dianne wrote a book, *Through the Dark Tunnel*, in which she told of her struggle, the horrific pain, the depression, and the slow recovery after being affected with polio. During her recovery of many months; she was assisted by dedicated doctors and therapists, and armed with determination, and strength from God. After about two years she was able to return to her husband, and two young daughters, but she had lost her ability to walk. Polio was the dreaded viral disease that crippled many young people in the 1940's and early 1950's. Only the fittest survived.

HAIR

Mama told me several times that I had curly hair when I was very young. She said she had cut it when I was around four. Then it grew straight, but she always kept it braided.

Throughout my grade school years, Mama would not cut my hair. She often stated, "Your hair is your crowning glory. It is a sin to cut it." She would not let me comb or brush it, but she kept it braided and when the braids were long enough, they were wrapped around my head, a style that made me look years older.

One day I had moved too much when she brushed and pulled my hair. Angrily she slapped the back of my left hand with that pin-bristled brush. The brush had pins, like sewing pins, instead of bristles. It was one of the attachments from her "magnetic healing machine." Oh! But that hurt! She had hit my hand so hard that every pin had penetrated my skin. My hand looked terrible with all of those little red pierce marks on it.

At school that day, I was questioned about the red dots on my hand. I was ashamed to let anyone know that I had been disobedient and had not sat still while my hair was being pulled. I sadly lied, "I fell into a sand bur patch."

* * *

Mama always chose a hot August day for my annual hair shampoo. I loved the feel of clean hair but I hated the annual shampoo because I had to sit out in the hot sun until my long hair was completely dry. She said, "You gota sit in the sun until your hair is dry so you won't git sick." The sun would be so hot in our yard surrounded by trees that I soon felt ill, dizzy, and like I could pass out. She'd watch to make sure I did not slip into the shade of the trees.

* * *

The summer I was 14, I was so disgusted because she would not let me even comb or brush my hair that I made up my mind to cut it. One day while Mama was taking her afternoon nap, I took the barber scissors from the medicine cabinet, went out into the pasture behind the cow barn, and cut my hair. I buried the cut off hair near a clump of sagebrush. I returned and quietly replaced the scissors. I had cut my hair with scissors. Usually when the ends of my braids were very uneven, Mama would burn the ends even with a match. "Burning would seal in the life of the hair and keep it from turning gray," she had stated.

When Mama saw me after her nap, I learned that I was the worst of sinners – I had sinned against God, my crowning glory had been destroyed!

56

At least now I was allowed to comb and brush my own shoulder-length hair. She said, "For that (sin) we would not be going to the State Fair in Lincoln." This was an annual event I had begged to attend. Even though I knew it was impossible because Mama would have been afraid to leave the farm.

Later she allowed me to have a permanent as short curly hair was the style. I had a machine perm. My hair was shampooed, parted, and rolled on rollers. It was saturated with a chemical solution that had a strong ammonia odor as the hair was rolled up. The solution was slathered on my hair, again just before the big clamps were applied. These clamps were attached to wires from the top of the machine. Then the electrical current was turned on and a timer set. Result: the hair retained a curl to fit the rollers, even after many shampoos. The rollers and clamps made my head very heavy during the processing.

I saw some of my classmates in town after the perm. Mama said, "You are too good to speak to them." How hateful! The next school day more critical remarks were made about me being "too high headed" to speak. If only they had known. Those girls were my friends.

FIGHTENED HORSES

One evening, at supper, E.B. said, "I want two horses taken to the northwest pasture." He looked at me and continued, "You can lead the horses. I'll follow with the car, stop, open the gate; then I'll release the horses before I pump water for the livestock."

It all sounded safe; Mama agreed that I could lead the gentle horses. I left with the two horses and held the ropes attached to the halter of each horse as I walked the quarter mile up the hill to the pasture gate by our rural mail box. I arrived at the gate a minute before I heard the roar of the car's motor as it rumbled up the hill. The horses reared and snorted. I was afraid that one of them would strike me with its hooves as it reared. E.B. stopped the car. Somehow in the turmoil, he got the gate open in time for the frightened horses to race away into the pasture still wearing their halters and lead ropes. In the confusion with the terrified, rearing horses, I was pulled into the barbed wire fence. The sharp barbs ripped two big gashes in my left side. Several days later he caught the horses and removed their halters and lead ropes.

I cried as I ran home holding my bleeding, hurting side. Mama bandaged my side with some clean white rags. The gashes left two long ugly scars and hurt for years. Mama said, "I had an uncomfortable feeling about you leading the horses."

She yelled some very harsh words at E.B. when he got home including, ". . .Elsieferne could've been killed!" He ignored her as usual, as he walked out the door.

SCHOOL POTPOURRI

(A collection of happenings during my grade school years, grades 1-8 at District #37.)

I completed grades one and two my first year in school with no problems. It was six weeks before I felt comfortable to talk. In grade three we had column addition in arithmetic. How I despised those problems! It was so much more interesting to watch the eighth graders solve square root problems on the blackboard. I always had answers for my addition problems but I had obtained the answers by looking at the long column of numbers and writing down a number for the answer. After Miss Stamn, my third grade teacher, graded my papers, she informed me, "You must write the number you carry to the next column at the top of that column."

"Oh," I thought, "I can do that, no problem." Using my usual method to obtain my answers, I'd look at the numbers and wrote a number in the answer space and a smaller number at the top of the column. I never received another negative comment about my addition problems. My thought—Were my papers graded? Answer: probably not.

* * *

My breakfast of half-cup of stewed tomatoes did not provide much stick-to-the-ribs-type nourishment. I was always so hungry as I walked to school that I would eat part of my lunch. When noon came I had only had part of my lunch, I was still so hungry. When I was in the third grade, at one afternoon recess the other children had opened their lunch buckets and took out delicious sugar cookies. That mouth-watering aroma made me feel famished. I could resist no longer. I opened one of their lunch buckets while they were all out on the playground, and took a cookie. What a wonderful heavenly taste! But one of the children recognized the cookie and immediately told Miss Stamn; she picked up a great big club and hit me. She never asked me where or why I had gotten the cookie. From then on I resisted the tantalizing aroma of the home-made sugar cookies, yet I was always hungry. By supper time (around

8 or 9 p.m.), I would be so hungry that I would overeat. My diet contained high quantities of fatty foods—fat meat, cream, and starches.

It was not unusual to awaken in the morning very dizzy and sick to my stomach and unable to do anything. In a little while I'd vomit up the most vile, bitter-tasting, green substance. A few minutes after I vomited, I'd feel fine. Mama called it a "bilious attack."

* * *

My walks to and from school were always interesting. Oh how I hated the cold wind and snow but spring and fall I never knew who or what I'd meet. One day I saw a coyote trying to catch a turkey for breakfast. The turkey family was under the only tree on my walk to school. The gobbler gobbled his loudest and strutted his finest steps to frighten the coyote. The hen signaled with clucks for the brown, fluffy babies to hide for their safety. Everyone was frightened even me as I ran the rest of the way to school. I don't know if the coyote had a tasty turkey breakfast or not.

* * *

Spring mornings I'd hear the meadow larks flute-like songs about spring while standing tall on the fence posts with their bright yellow breasts puffed out accented by their brown backs, black vests and yellow throats. I loved their songs. Occasionally I'd hear a prairie chicken "booming" its mating ritual.

Another time I heard a noise to my left. I looked to see what was nearby but saw nothing but a zig-zagged trail in the sand. Looking to my right I finally saw a black or dark blue snake racing away from me. I thought it could aptly be called a "racer."

Spring flowers were always welcomed. I loved the sweet aroma of wild purple sweet peas. The yellow prickery pear blossoms were gorgeous, as were the deep rose flowers of the pin cushion cactus.

* * *

Spelling Bees were a frequently activity that was enjoyed by all the students. Each grade was given words of their own grade level. One year I was the top speller in the school. I do not recall whether it was seventh or eighth grade. I received an award, a little book, *Memory Gems*, fifth edition, by Sam G. Stephenson (1924 – price 50 cents). I was the District 37 representative to the county Spelling Bee in Benkelman.

I worked hard on the long lists of words so I would do well. I had very little help from Mama as her reading skills were very limited. My parents

59

took me to the event. It was held at the County Court house; I don't recall for certain but think it was held in the court room. I was nervous as there were so many people present. I survived several rounds, but than nerves got the best of me. I missed "kerosene" a word I knew how to spell. I was happy that I had had that opportunity.

*　*　*

The boys at school were frequently picking on me as a target for their mischievous behavior. This incident happened the year our school was invited to participate in a program at the nearby Hoover School. Everyone was excited and working on the assigned parts.

My special friend, Luella Keene and I, were fourth graders. We liked to spend recess time together but we had to hide in the girls' toilet building to keep away from the boys. The boys had brought their lariats to school and during recess tried to improve their skill. As Luella and I ran to the girls' toilet building, I was caught with the lariat. The rope caught my left arm and pulled my sleeve up above my elbow. It burned my bare arm as I was dragged across the school ground. My arm bled from large rope burns.

When I got home that night, Mama saw my arm. After she learned about the accident, she stated, "We'll show them. You ain't goin' to the Hoover School for that stupid program." I felt Mama did not love me when she punished me because I had been hurt. Punishment for the lariat owners? I was never aware of any but the lariats never appeared at school again.

*　*　*

After one of our many snows, Carl brought his sled to school. The boys' toilet-coal- shed combination building was located on the largest rise on the school ground. The snow on the path was well packed and made a perfect sledding slope. Carl shared his sled with all the children. I was allowed one ride down the hill then I sadly watched the other children have fun. But what fun my first and only sled ride was! I do not recall seeing the sled at school again.

*　*　*

On the last day of school of my first year in school, we had a pitch-in dinner at noon. Mama sent me with an apple pie baked with very little sugar and peelings still on the apples. I took it back home untouched. Mama refused to go with me; her excuse—"I ain't fit to be seen." It was a bountiful dinner and enjoyed by all on the bright sunny day in late April.

Another year we went to "Old Baldy" a very sandy hill about eight miles away. "Old Baldy" was a grassless, big, sandy hill in the pasture on Wynona's parent's farm. Wynona's parents were our neighpors. It was so much fun to try to walk or run while sinking up to our ankles, and knees in the soft sand. A fun way to end the school year.

* * *

I recall that Donna's mom was the only parent who visited school. She brought Donna to school each day and picked her up each evening. It was very unusual as all the other students either walked or rode a horse on a regular basis. Donna lived three miles from school. After Donna's baby sister arrived, her little sister was the grand attraction at the school when her mama visited.

* * *

Birdena Boswell was my eighth grade teacher. The student body had decreased to just nine students from the 32 the first year I was in school. I worked hard and made good grades, that I felt would be needed to go to high school in the fall. My brothers had gone directly to high school after graduating from the eighth grade. I expected to do the same. I had passed the state tests with A's, B's, and one C+, on a three point scale. I thought Mama was pleased.

Mrs. Boswell announced in April that Katie Logan, our County School Superintendent would visit the next day. When I arrived home, I relayed the news of Katie Logan's expected visit. Mama's words were, "You tell that Katie Logan that you won't graduate this year. You have to take the eighth grade over; you have to do better." Words could not express my shock, sadness, disappointment, and disbelief. I had tried so hard but just could not please Mama. I had failed to be perfect. I had completed the eight grades in seven years. "Why?" I softly questioned, "Do I have to repeat the eighth grade?"

I dutifully relayed Mama's expectations to Mrs. Logan, but she quickly replied, "You tell your Mama that you **will** receive your diploma this year. You have passed all of your classes with good grades. You deserve your diploma and you will receive it." I carried the news home. Mama wasn't happy. Carl, Linn, Dale and I represented the eighth grade graduating class of 1938 from District #37. My diploma arrived in the mail after the county graduation exercises had been held.

True to her decision, I had to repeat the eighth grade the following school year. Did I work to raise my grades? Why bother? I had my diploma; I had graduated. Mrs. Boswell was the teacher again. She let me help younger students and work on pictures for the art exhibit at the county fair. I received several blue and red ribbons. I routinely turned in class work and even took the state tests again. Grades? Same as the previous year.

* * *

I met my seventh grade teacher, over 60 years after she'd been my teacher. In our conversation, I casually mentioned that I had to take the eighth grade over. "Why? She questioned, "You were one of the best students I had." Those were wonderful words to hear.

* * *

Years later I learned Mrs. Boswell lived in a retirement home in Mesa, Arizona. I wrote and asked if she remembered me. Her reply was that indeed she remembered me as she related:

> "You were the girl with a very long first name. The space on the report card for the student's name was small. I wrote just 'Elsief.' When I picked up my first check at your house, your mother gave me the understanding that leaving part of your name off your report card was unacceptable." She continued, "You were the girl who wore a little bag of asafetida." (She reminded me of that fowl, smelling, herb root that Mama would order from an herb catalogue and make me wear in a bag around my neck to ward off germs even when I was 14 years old.)

> Mrs. Boswell and I exchanged letters until her health failed.

FARM WORK

(This section briefly describes the farm work I was required to do during my second year in the eighth grade.)

I helped my dad grind grain and other feed in the hammer mill for the livestock immediately after the morning chores were done. We ground ear corn to feed the horses and chickens. Other times we ground corn stalks with the ears attached for cow feed. This was like grain and hay combined. E.B. took care of the ground feed from the mill. Feeding the hopper of the whirling blades of the hammer mill was a dangerous job for a young teenager as there no safety shields. By 8:30 a.m., we quit; I'd washed my face and changed clothes. Then E.B. would take me to school. It wasn't too much bother when I was working for him. In the afternoon, I'd walk home.

* * *

Mama and I took a team of horses and a wagon with a "throw board," an extension of boards on one side of the wagon to keep the ears of corn thrown at the wagon from going over the wagon. We would pick half a wagon load of corn for hog feed. The ear corn would be scattered on the ground. The hogs hungrily fought for it.

* * *

Native grass or prairie hay was harvested in August. After it had been cut and dried, I helped load the wagon with loose hay. It was hauled to the barnyard and stacked into stacks for winter feed for the livestock. When I was 14 or 15, I stacked a haystack by myself. Building a haystack with loose hay is a challenging task. My hay stack had a slight sway on one side but did not fall down.

Mama and I feeding calves milk from buckets.

*Six-horse team stands
at attention beside
the Author*

*The Author holding paws of
Tippy, the farm dog*

PART III

HIGH SCHOOL

FRESHMAN YEAR - 1940-41

Summer was passing quickly. I talked about high school. Mama would say, "We'll see." That was only a thin thread of hope, but I refused to give up. I wanted to attend high school. I felt I should be given the same privilege as my brothers as they both attended high school. I even tried to take classes by correspondence. The books were ordered from the University of Nebraska, Lincoln, Nebraska. How disappointing to find the books so difficult I could not understand them! Crying silently, I boxed the books up and we returned them.

Early in August 1940, a strange car pulled into our driveway. An older gentleman got out and came to the door. Mama wondered aloud, "Who is that guy and what does he want? Ellis is out in the field." Mama answered the door. The gent introduced himself as Sam G. from Parks. He said that he had purchased a small school bus, and was signing up students for a bus route to Parks High School. (Parks High was one of the smaller county high schools and the closest to my home.) Most of our roads were sand and dirt, but the roads nearer to Parks were graded and topped with gravel. A small bus, about the size of a regular farm truck, could safely travel on these roads. The route would be a thirty-mile ride each way. Sam said that on the nights when there were after school activities; the bus would bring the students home after the activity.

Mama agreed. She no longer had an excuse to keep me home as I would be home every night. The bus would pick me up at my house. My enthusiasm soared yet I hid my euphoric feelings. I could hardly believe that my dream could become a reality. I wanted to shout "Yes, at last!" This meant that my morning chores had to be done very early as I had to be ready for the bus by 7 a.m.

Mama surprised me "You will need some new clothes. You may pick out a dress, slip, wool skirt, and sweater from the Sears sale catalogue." I chose a light green, floral designed, short-sleeved dress, a medium blue, circular wool skirt, and a sweater. She also said, "We will buy fabric to make two blouses and two skirts." She chose lightweight white and yellow shiny rayon fabric. She said I had to wear silks and satins because of this story that had been told by Mike Grams, her father, my grandfather:

> My grandfather was a high lord in Germany, who liked to gamble. He gambled away his fortune, lost his home, and even lost his lordship. He took his family and fled to Prussia. When my father, Mike Grams, was old enough to be in the Russian Army, the family returned to Germany to keep Mike out of the army.

Later research revealed that Mike Grams had proudly served in the Russian Army for five years. That story was the reason Mama said I was royalty and had to wear silks and satins; it was repeated so often during my growing up years that the message became an old broken record.

We made a skirt and short-sleeved blouse of each color of the rayon fabrics. Later I was allowed to select my first new winter coat from the special fall Sears sale catalogue. Wool winter coats were $5.00 with no choice of style or color. When the coat arrived, it was maroon colored. That year Aunt Susan sent me a bright red beret for Christmas. My coat and beret were not the best color combination, but I had no other choice, and dared not to complain.

The first Monday of September the little yellow school bus arrived at the appointed time. About half of the seats were taken. I recognized two of the girls who had graduated in May from my school. None of the three boys of my graduate class were on the bus.

The bus arrived at the Parks School a few minutes before nine o'clock. It was a two-story red brick building for all 12 grades. Grades 1-4 were in one room on the first floor. Also on the first floor was the room designed to be the Home Economics room, but occupied by the boys' shop class (woodworking – just for boys – no girls allowed), the gymnasium for boys' basketball, the furnace room, and the rest rooms. The Benkelman, Nebraska power plant located 15 miles away furnished the electricity.

On the second floor, directly above the room for the lower grades, was the room for grades 5-8. The high school had three classrooms and a large study hall. All the students kept their books in their desks in the study hall as there were no lockers. The school paper was published each month. It was typed on a stencil then copies were made on a mimeograph machine. Our library consisted of 150 novels and one reference book, an unabridged Webster's Dictionary that was kept on pedestal table in the study hall.

The faculty members were: Mr. Kolb, superintendent, Mr. Sutherland, principal and Miss Reger. Mr. Kolb taught several classes including freshman general science, and woodworking. Mr. Sutherland taught math classes, bookkeeping, shorthand, typing, and coached. Miss Reger taught English literature, grammar, Latin, and history, also supervised the newsletter, and was cheerleader coach, and chorus director.

The school consisted of 60 students with fourteen students in my 1940 Freshmen Class. A school rule was that all students who had an A average for the semester were exempt from final semester tests. I took no final tests the first semester.

The bus ride was not a pleasant experience for me. First, the boys would get into my lunch bucket if I put it into the overhead rack. One evening they retrieved my lunch bucket, without my knowledge, and found the long stockings that I had removed and stowed away. What a laugh they had to my embarrassment! I felt they had no business with my lunch pail. The bus driver never appeared to be aware of any misbehavior on the bus.

Parks had a six-man football team. These games were played immediately after school. At the first football game, I was astounded as the boys rammed into each other without a thought as to what happened to the other player. One boy received a bloody nose. That game didn't look like much fun.

The annual Freshman Initiation Week occurred soon after the beginning of school. All members of the Freshmen Class were requested to dress differently for the entire week before the Friday night party. One year the boys had to wear women's hats and an apron, roll up their pant legs, and carry a toy. While the girls wore boy's pants or overalls, a boy's cap, boy's shoes, false whiskers or a mustache, and carry a boy's toy. I do not recall what ridiculous garb we were supposed to wear for that week. I was not allowed to dress as requested.

Next was the Party! I had never been to a party. This was during the era when all girls and women wore dresses or skirts. Elaine, a sophomore, told me I should wear slacks to the party as the boys would pull my skirt up. "I have no slacks because Mama won't allow me to wear pants." I replied. She said that her mother had an old pair of slacks and a matching blouse that I could wear. She brought them to the school. Before the party, I changed into them as I certainly did not want anyone pulling up my skirt!

The Sophomore Class sponsored the special initiation activities. Basketball was played before the party games. I thought why not join in the fun and play basketball with the girls? I wanted so much to be part of the group, not a wallflower always looking on while others had fun. This was about ten days after I had received my smallpox vaccination. The hard, indented, crusty scab was firm on my upper left arm. After about three minutes of play, one of the girl's elbows accidentally came down hard on my arm, hitting that scab. WOW! What a searing pain! I was nauseated; tears rolled. I sat down with my bleeding arm. My basketball playing ended.

The first of the traditional initiation activities was the "electric chair." I was the first "victim." A scarf was placed over my eyes to blindfold me after I sat down on the required metal folding chair. Then I heard the remorseful comment, "She's wearing slacks." Elaine's warning had been verified. I was so thankful that she had offered her mother's slacks for me to wear.

A wash pan with some water in it was set on my lap, and I was requested to place my hands in the water. Either my hands or the water was to be touched with a bare copper wire connected to two large dry cell batteries to give a "shock." I don't know what prompted me to flip my water-soaked fingers while they were connecting the wires to the batteries, but I did. The flying water evidently fell on the batteries. "She flipped water on the batteries. Now they won't work!" lamented the Sophomore Class boys who were to "throw" the electric switch. I recall no more "electric chair executions." I wondered if the sophomores were disappointed or if I were the only chosen "victim" for the "electric chair." I may have spoiled their fun, but I smiled to myself. I do not recall the other games that were played.

After the party, I changed back into my dress and neatly folded the borrowed slacks and blouse. I wanted to take them home to launder and press, but knew I did not dare to follow the proper etiquette rules. I was ashamed, but I did not want to be told that I had sinned because I had worn pants. I could not understand what was so terribly wrong with wearing slacks. I wanted to avoid the scolding and criticism, which I had grown so weary of hearing. I returned the slacks and top to Elaine with thanks.

Early in December, both my lower wisdom teeth tried to emerge at the same time. My gums were swollen and infected. The swelling was so bad that I could hardly move my tongue. Eating was nearly impossible. Mama went with me to see the dentist. He said, "You need to go to a doctor."

We went to the doctor. He said, "This is a job for a dentist." No help. I continued to suffer.

Mama decided to treat my sore swollen gums and throat with her famous camphor gum-turpentine liniment. She rubbed it on my neck, and then tied a white cloth around my neck. (This liniment was made using a ten-cent square cake of camphor gum dissolved in a cup of turpentine or coal oil. It was used for sprains, sore throats, colds, and even rattlesnake bites on our milk cows.) What a "perfume" for me to wear to school! I never considered missing school. I could not blame the students for their unkind remarks. I could do nothing but listen and ignore with unshed tears.

I started to drive the car in December; I was just 15. Mama and I attended Sunday school on Sunday mornings for the first time in my life. The American Sunday School Union, an outreach program of the United Presbyterian Church, organized a Sunday school at the Rollwitz Church, which was four miles from my home. Previously there had been no religious leadership at the church for years. The Sunday school was great. I was finally able to be with my peers which I enjoyed very much. A semi-retired United Presbyterian minister, Rev. Foster drove 25 miles from Benkelman, Nebraska once a month to hold a worship service on a Sunday afternoon.

A Youth Group was organized and Oliver, a 48-year-old bachelor, was included. We had meetings once a month at different members' homes. Mama attended these local meetings with me, the same as several of the other mothers. She kept criticizing my behavior until I felt I could do nothing right. I was ready to scream, "Let me be, just once."

One very memorable party was a Halloween party with a haunted house built in the family's musty, smelling, empty fruit cellar. Shaking hands with a ghost, the haunting noises, and "spider webs" were all so much fun. Even the mothers enjoyed the festivities. These were first such festivities Mama had never been privileged to attend.

In January after my sixteenth birthday, I accompanied E.B. to Benkelman with plans get my driver's license. I was dropped off at the courthouse. I said, "I'll need the car for the driving test." My words were ignored as he quickly sped away. After I met the Deputy Sheriff, I searched all over town to find the car. I passed the written and driving tests and received my driver's license.

Second semester algebra became a challenge. The stress on the morning and evening bus ride affected my studies. I took my first final exam in algebra and passed. During the second semester, more malicious remarks were made directly to me, and behind my back, especially on the bus. I dreaded the bus ride more each week. The ridicule from my peers, especially the boys, was difficult to endure and ignore. But I endured.

The boys often referred to my clothes. One dress they called "your wedding dress." It was an old blue acetate crepe dress given to Mama. She covered the red fade streaks down the front with two three-inch wide strips of fancy ivory lace. She said, "This is good enough for you to wear." I did, just once. Many other cruel remarks were circulated both on the bus and at school. Those remarks made me feel I had no right to live or to attend school.

To celebrate Valentine's Day, a formal party was planned. The girls were to wear formals, a garment that I did not have. Mama said, "We'll make a formal with the sheer kitchen curtains." The curtains were taken down, laundered, starched and ironed. She sewed the top of the curtains together for the shoulder seams with an opening for my head. The curtain side seams became the side seams of "my dress." She asked me to cut out some red construction paper hearts. She tacked one on each shoulder, and then added a border of smaller hearts near the bottom. I wore a wide red ribbon sash. We found a long, pink, bias-cut, satin night gown to use as the slip. It cost one dollar. Mama was proud of her creation but it hardly fit in with the formals the other girls wore. This was my first long dress; it cost nothing. After the party, the dress again became kitchen curtains.

In the spring enroute home on the bus as I sat quietly in my seat, minding my own business, Francis, one of the bigger sophomore boys, got up from his seat at the back of the bus and walked several steps forward while the bus was moving. He stopped just behind my isle seat, doubled up his fist, and slammed it down onto the base of my neck as hard as he could. WOW! The stars were too numerous to count! My neck hurt and hot tears overflowed my eyes.

I told Mama when I got home. "You write to the State School Superintendent at Lincoln, Nebraska. You can writ' better than me as I ain't got no education," she stated. I did as she had requested but I felt out of place writing that letter.

About two weeks after my letter was mailed, I was called into Mr. Kolb's office. I was so frightened. "What have I done?" I kept asking myself as I trembled slowly into his office. Mr. Kolb stated that he had heard from the State Superintendent about Francis hitting me. I was even more anxious. He asked, "Why didn't you come to me to talk about it?"

Remorsefully, I said, "Mama told me to write the letter to the State Superintendent. I had no idea what to do." I was never asked if Sam, the bus driver, kept order on the bus. Mr. Kolb went on the say that he had talked to bus driver, Sam. And he admitted that he was unable to keep order on the bus. From that time on I was afraid to tell anyone about problems on the bus. It seemed better to accept the events and ignore them with unshed tears and keep everything to myself. I had to follow Mama's rule – **Don't rock the boat—let the others rule**.

Mama and I were going to a Sunday evening Youth group meeting. When we were a half-mile from home, smoke began billowing from underneath the car's hood. I stopped the car, turned off the switch, jumped out, raised the hood, and yanked off all the spark plug wires. Smoke continued its upward spiral. I suddenly realized I needed to disconnect cables from the battery that was located beneath the floor board under the driver's feet. I quickly grabbed the floor mat and floor board panel out and disconnected one of the battery cables. The smoke stopped. I was so frightened that I shook inside like a leaf. I was so scared because Mama had roared when Dad bought the car without her knowledge. I certainly did not want to hear her yell again if it burned.

I walked back to the house and told my dad what had happened and asked him to pull the car back home with a team and wagon. "Git the log chain," he requested. I did while he harnessed the horses and hitched them to a wagon. We soon had the car back home. I do not recall his words when I first broke the news to him about the fire.

Several days later Lyle came home for a visit. I asked him to reconnect the wires. After he worked on the rewiring, he asked "Sis, why did you pull all of the spark plug wires off? I had a terrible time trying to get them correctly replaced. You really did a good job of making a mess of the wiring."

I replied, "I did not want the car to burn up."

That was the second time Lyle repaired the car after I had damaged it. I was 14 and had washed the car. As I attempted to drive the car into the car shed I did not want get too close to the wall on the driver's side so I kept the driver's door open. Before I realized it, the V-8 Ford's front door, which opened from the front, had caught the car shed door frame. I had bent the door hinges before I got the car stopped. The next time when Lyle visited, he was asked to fix the hinges. He said, "That's no big problem." He quickly bent the hinges back to the original shape, and we could close the door. At times he was the nicest big brother any little sister could have.

During April 1941, rain fell for days. This was very unusual in this part of Nebraska, which normally had very little annual rainfall. The rain had washed holes in the sand and dirt roads; some roads were impassible. The Parks area was flooded from the creek that flowed through the village. School was held but my bus could not safely make the trip. It was up to the parents to transport their children. E.B. took me to school that morning. As I exited the car I said, "Stop at Leanna's home before you drive past as I may be able to get a ride to her place." I did not have an opportunity to ask Leanna for ride to her home. Also, Mama's words – "You are **never** to ride with anyone." still echoed in my mind. Yet I felt confident that he would come for me, if I were not at her home.

After school, I waited and waited at the school building. The school building closed so I walked to the Kulhman's grocery store about a block from the school. It was getting late. I didn't know what to do. We had no telephone so I could not phone home, but he never came.

Finally, Mrs. Kulhman, who knew my parents, realized my dilemma and said; "You can stay with us tonight." I had no place to go, no money to buy food. I was hungry. I felt abandoned, betrayed. I'd never been away from home alone over night. Tears kept me company as I tried to be brave. Mrs. Kulhman, said, "You can go down to our home in the basement. It is time to close for the night. I'll be down in a few minutes."

I turned on the electric light then slowly walked down the steps to their home under their store. First, I saw the living room. It was so warm and cozy with rugs on the floor, the beautiful furniture, an old-fashioned foot pedal parlor organ (similar to the one we had at home), and a bookcase of books. I stopped at the organ and was tempted to try to play it yet I was afraid to touch it.

I looked in the kitchen at the cabinets, the stove, the table and chairs, all so fresh and clean. I did not explore the bedroom. I was very timid, shy, afraid, lonesome, and sad. I did not know what to do. I felt so out of place in this lovely home – I didn't belong here.

Soon Mrs. Kulhman came downstairs and started to prepare supper. I offered to help and set the table. She said that Mr. Kulhman would come in a few minutes after he had locked the store. We had a tasty supper and soon prepared for bed. She made up a half-bed that set in the hallway near the living room and provided me with a gown. I tried to sleep but could not—fear, sorrow, tears, anger, disappointment, and abandonment all kept my mind in turmoil. The next day I wore the same garments to school as I had the previous day, which wasn't unusual.

The next morning Mrs. Kulhman prepared breakfast. We all went upstairs. "Be sure to come back for lunch," she said as I walked out the door enroute to school.

By the end of school, the roads had been repaired. I rode the bus home. I questioned E.B. as to why he had not come for me, "You said you'd be at Leanna's home. I went there and you weren't there. I don't have time to run all over the county for you. I don't have time to run after you." he stated angrily.

More silent unshed tears. I dared not say anything. Everywhere I turned no one really wanted me.

I now understood that he did not hear or chose not to hear me say, "I **may** be able to get a ride part way home." I was so confused. I knew E.B. did not care about me. Mama demanded I do things she should have done. I needed someone to talk with but there was no one. I was so confused and wondered what I would ever be able to do.

The school year ended. I was so thankful I had been able to begin to realize my dream, but I was apprehensive about the next three years after so much harassment this year.

SOPHOMORE YEAR – 1941-42

During August, prior to school, Mama and I searched in Parks for a place for me to stay during the new school year. Parks was a very small village. Few homes accepted student boarders.

We finally found Mrs. Knepper, an elderly lady who lived alone and had an extra bedroom. Her house was about a block from the school, and next door to Elaine, the girl who had befriended me before the Freshman Initiation Party.

Mrs. Kneeper's home consisted of a living room and two bedrooms upstairs. The kitchen, pantry, and dining room were in the basement. The back door opened to an outside stairway that was covered with a slanted door (the type used for root or storm cellars). Water was available from an inside pump. Lights were kerosene lamps. The rest room was an outside privy—still common in that era. The upstairs was heated with an oil heating stove; the basement with the kitchen range. I was delighted not to have to ride the bus every day, but I did take my small cardboard suitcase and rode to school on Monday morning and home on Friday evening.

Mr. Sutherland was the school superintendent. He taught several classes, especially the business classes, and coached. Mrs. Reger, principal, taught Latin, English classes, junior business, and creative English. Mrs. Ough, a new teacher, taught civics, biology, and world history.

The school did not own typewriters. Typing students could rent typewriters provided by a company in McCook, Nebraska. These were reconditioned office typewriters that were kept at the school for the school year. Mama decided that rent for a typewriter would soon pay for one. We were able to purchase a new portable typewriter with pica type for $40.00. I could take my typewriter home anytime. Pins were awarded for typing speeds. I was able to earn a 40-word-per-minute bronze pin. Some students earned the 60-word gold pins.

School classes went quite well but a new problem surfaced. Mrs. Knepper evidently had very poor eyesight. She served cold cereal for breakfast. In the cereal were many small black rice-sized additions. What a disappointment! She frequently served a tasty dish, Spanish rice, for supper. Again those black rice-sized additions were in the rice. Scavenger mice lived high in her pantry. The open boxes of cereals and rice on the shelves provided a bountiful feast. My appetite suffered. Yet neither she nor I became ill. She had probably eaten the same basic food all the time she lived in that house. The slanted back door to the basement stairs did not fit tight, neither did the inside upright door. The traps she had used to catch the mice were ineffective. In the night, I even heard them rummage in the upstairs waste paper basket.

I talked to Mama about the food. We did not have fancy food at home but never had the food been invaded by mice. I avoided the worst of the unwanted items as much as possible but Monday noon through Friday noon that was my diet. I was always happy when Friday came.

Mrs. Knepper was a basketball fan and went to every home game. Culture shock hit me when I attended the first basketball game. I was astounded to see the team wearing brief uniform shorts and sleeveless shirts. Quite a surprise for this sandpiper, who had seen men wear only long sleeved shirts and long pants. Those players looked undressed, like they were wearing their colored underwear!

The Parks Community Club met once a month at the Community Building. Everyone looked forward to the bountiful pitch-in meal that was followed by socializing, and square and folk dancing. Since dancing was a sin, I didn't tell Mama much about it. The Grand March was my favorite. Young and old participated in the dancing. Mrs. Knepper and I were regular attendees.

Mama often went with my dad to the Thursday livestock auction barn in Benkelman. Besides the auctioning of cattle, horses, and hogs, farm machinery, and other miscellaneous items, there were truck loads of produce direct from the producers. According to the season many fruits and vegetables, plus gallon cans of sorghum, syrup and honey were available.

One Saturday after Mama had been at the Thursday livestock auction, she said that she had over heard some women talk about the length of my dresses because they were longer than hers. I said to myself, "So what! Can't I wear my dresses whatever length I please without you criticizing me?" My dresses were the same length as my classmates. Then I wondered, "Why are you telling me this? Do you want me to think that everyone is criticizing me like you do?" I considered her message as gossip. I silently pondered, "Why is it their business the length I wear my skirts?" To me this was nothing but gossip. I wondered if Mama had invented it.

I went to the school roller skating parties that were held once each semester. We traveled 15 miles by school bus to the nearest roller skating rink at Benkelman, Nebraska. Skating was fun yet I had no idea how to skate. No suggestions or help was offered. I was so clumsy on the skates. I realized everyone else frequently enjoyed this activity that was never available to me. I don't know if roller-skating was a "sin" or not. I fell so much that I hurt both wrists as I tried to catch myself. They hurt for months after skating but I did not dare mention that to Mama, as I did not want her to forbid me from attending high school.

Around 2:00 o'clock the morning, after the spring skating party, I was awakened by unusual outside noises in this quiet village. I opened my eyes and saw a reddish glow in my east window. It was difficult to understand what I heard and saw. I went into the living room where I could see that the red glow was everywhere. Mrs. Knepper was up and said, "The Loveland house (about a half block away) at the corner was burning." We quickly dressed and went outside, but we could see nothing but the flames and many people were standing around. It was terrifying.

Loveland's daughter, who attended the skating party, arrived home around 11:00 p.m. It was reported that she had lit a match to light a lamp, and had thrown the flameless black match into the cob box. Shucks were on the cobs, and the match head had enough heat to smolder until it flamed. Soon the whole house was engulfed. Everyone got out safely but the family lost everything. That was the first time I had ever seen a building on fire. Little could be done to control the fire, as there was no water or fire fighting equipment.

The wooden shingle-covered walls of the Cox home next door were wet from the rain that had fallen the day before that helped protect this house from catching fire. The neighbors worked diligently to make sure the fire was contained to the one house on the corner.

My first year in high school was very discouraging since I was the subject of so much unfriendly peer pressure and bullying especially on the bus. The second year the food was so disgusting. Either one would have been enough to discourage some, but not me. I was determined to get my high school diploma. I was so hungry for knowledge. Now I silently vowed to graduate the next year.

JUNIOR – SENIOR YEAR – 1942-43

August 1942, Mama and I searched in Parks for a different place for me to live during my third year of high school. No place was available. We returned to Mrs. Knepper and learned that she had rented "my room" to the new school superintendent, Mrs. Davidson.

Disappointment showed on my face then Mrs. Kepper realized I had expected to stay with her again. She suggested "You can stay in the basement. There is a day bed in the dining room that you can sleep on and a lantern-type kerosene heater for heat." I accepted the only choice I had. How I dreaded mealtime! But that was my only choice. Now I would share food and space with the mice.

The teaching staff had completely changed. Mrs. Davidson was school superintendent, Mrs. Inez Tecker, principal, and Mrs. Hester, a teacher. Our country was involved in WWII. Teachers were scarce. The electives changed but the required subjects were still taught. The popular electives: typing, shorthand, and bookkeeping were no longer offered. I had planned to take shorthand and bookkeeping but that was no longer possible.

It was the custom for the Senior Class and their sponsor, to plan a short trip out of town, for "Senior Sneak Days." The object was to leave the school community without the student body knowing when or where the Senior Class had gone. Rumors in the war-related news predicted gas rationing as a coming reality. The eight-member Senior Class with their sponsor, Miss Hunter, planned their "Sneak" for the fall instead of the spring to avoid the gas rationing. The class took their trip in October.

The fourth week of October school met only three days. The State required all teachers to attend the annual two-day training called "Teachers Institute." I drove to school to sell eggs to Kulhman's grocery store, and deliver a five-gallon can of cream to the railroad station to be shipped to the creamery at Hastings, Nebraska. Mama said, "You must put the car in storage at the Leach Garage. No one will damage it when it's out of sight." I did as asked.

Tuesday night, I was standing by the small lantern-type heater in my basement room with no light except the light provided by the kerosene heater, taking a quick sponge bath, when I heard voices at the basement window above and behind me. I turned my head to look up at the window, and then I heard sounds and vibrations of running feet. The "window peepers" saw only my robed back. I quickly ran upstairs and told Mrs. Knepper. Her reply, "Oh, you are just hearing things. There are no boys around here that would be window peeping." Nervously, I went back downstairs, turned out the heater, finished my bath, and went to bed still frightened. The back door was never locked.

The next morning I walked around the house to check for tracks, as I knew I had heard someone at that window. The light snowfall of the previous day revealed several large footprints right by my basement window, and depressed footprints by the nearby fence showing that someone had jumped over it. I reported my sightings to Mrs. Knepper. Did she believe me? I do not recall her response.

Mrs. Davidson did not remain long as one of Mrs. Knepper's boarders. Soon I had my old room back. I had hoped for a change of food during Mrs. Davidson's presence but there was none.

I took five subjects each semester to earn extra credits. The graduation requirements at that time were 28 credits minimum, or 32 maximum. I knew I could earn at least 28 credits. I reasoned that would not be bad in three years. A rumor was circulating around the school that I was going to graduate in the spring of 1943.

Class rings were a **must.** I had been permitted to order a ring during the second semester of my sophomore year engraved with the projected date of my graduation. When the rings arrived in the fall of 1942, Elaine immediately insisted on seeing my ring. She had heard the rumor circulating of my possible graduation with her class but she could see the date on my ring was 1944, while the date on her ring was 1943. Things went on quietly for weeks. I was easily passing my five classes.

I was still active in the Youth Group at church. I enjoyed being with my peers. In December, youth groups from several area churches were invited for a special meeting at a small church about 20 miles away in the northwest part of the county. Two weeks before the event, Oliver, the 48-year-old bachelor, asked if he could take me. Immediately I told him, "No!"

Mama had not accompanied me that Sunday morning. I told her of Oliver's request, and said I told him, "No."

She said, "You tell him, he can take you." I was flabbergasted. I thought she would be proud of me for saying, "No" as she had said I was too busy to date. Before Oliver came, she gave me an understanding that this was not a "**date.**"

It was most difficult for me to change my answer. Actually I felt like a fool when I did, I felt as if I were doing something very, very wrong. I wanted so much to be with my peers. Oliver came early, and we parked by the church to wait for the others to come as the group was car-pooling. He would not keep his hands off me until I threaten to get out of his car and walk home. Finally he agreed to behave himself. Later he asked me to several different activities. Each time I said, "No!" And I **never** told Mama.

Ernest Graham, one of the young men of the community, was called into the service for our country. The youth group had a going away party for him at Oliver's home. Oliver lived with his parents and spinster sister. When I asked to go, Mama said, "No, they will probably be playing cards. That is a sin." Again my heart silently sank.

The second semester, a librarian was needed at my school. I volunteered. I was to have an assistant but she showed no interest in checking out the books. I handled the checking out of our 150 novels and as the sole librarian I kept the cards in my desk.

One Saturday morning in the spring, Mama surprised me, "We are going to see *Gone with the Wind.* It was the new movie that had begun to circulate to the small theatres. She said, "You need to do some of the things other young people are doing." I had heard so many times that movies were sinful. I wasn't sure I could trust her words. She and I attended the movie at the Zorn Theatre in Benkelman. I do not recall that my dad accompanied us.

I was so impressed with the movie *Gone with the Wind* in color that I asked my English teacher if I could write a book report on it. Our 150-volume library did not contain that new book. I said, "I have seen the movie; I did not read book." I was pleased when she allowed me to write the report.

Positive rumors continued to circulate around the school about my graduation. Elaine and I were both going to teach in one-room schools in the fall. I already had my contract. Parks High did not offer "normal training" for teaching. That meant we would need to attend summer school. We were enrolled at the McCook Junior College 60 miles away where in 10 weeks we could earn 12 hours of credit and receive a conditional three-year teaching certificate.

Mrs. Davidson had allowed Elaine to tutor eighth grade students. I was helping Miss Hunter in grades 1-4, during the time that Miss Hunter worked with the Junior/Senior classes for play practice. The Nebraska school rules stated that all tutoring by unlicensed aides must be in the presence of a licensed teacher. This meant tutoring should be done within the classroom. It was known all over the community that Elaine would take the eighth grade student that she was tutoring into an empty classroom.

The next thing I knew was I was summoned into Mrs. Davidson's office. "What now?" I puzzled. I am working very hard to keep up my grades. I did not take a part in the Junior-Senior play "Arsenic and Old Lace" instead I worked with the ticket sales, and substituted in Miss Hunter's Classroom while she directed the play cast.

Mrs. Davidson immediately stated, "You have been telling all over town that Elaine has been tutoring outside the classroom. Now you will lose your half of the scholarship to McCook Junior College." Mrs. Davidson had promised me half of that $25.00 scholarship. What a shock that was! It was like a hard slap in my face! I had not even thought about telling people something that was common knowledge.

That evening I told Mrs. Knepper about the loss of my half the scholarship. "Why?" she questioned "Everyone in town knows what Elaine is doing. You did nothing wrong." At least one person was on my side. Again I was punished for something of which I was not guilty.

Why?" I questioned, "Does everyone seem to be against me? Why?

Elaine was named valedictorian and received the $25.00 scholarship. I had lost my half of it without doing anything wrong. I was not given a chance to tell Mrs. Davidson that I had not acted as I had been accused. I was heart broken. It was so unfair.

Six weeks before school was out, the Junior Class met to plan the Junior-Senior banquet. It was the tradition that the Junior Class planned the banquet to honor the Senior Class. I was asked to resign my job as treasurer of the Junior Class. Now I was officially the ninth member of the Senior Class.

May 2, brought heart breaking news to my family—my brother, Lyle had drowned at the Imperial, Nebraska City Reservoir where he and two buddies had been fishing. Lyle, an excellent swimmer, had stated he would race them to the other side of the reservoir then jumped into the cold water to swim across to the other side. The other men could not swim. Lyle sank and never surfaced. He was just 26 years old and was survived by his wife and their four year-old daughter.

After that sad news on Sunday evening, Mama let me take the bus to school on Monday morning to report to the teachers, get my assignments, and my typewriter. I rode the bus home that night. So many sarcastic remarks were made by several of the students about my brother that it was heartbreaking. I could not understand why a death in the family could draw such cruel remarks. Mama would not let me return to school for a whole week after the funeral. I began to wonder if she would let me graduate.

Alvin lived in California; he came for Lyle's funeral. The next day after the funeral, we took Alvin to North Platte, Nebraska to catch the Union Pacific Zephyr to California. Since I had not been a member of the Senior Class when the other class members had photos taken, I was requested to get a studio portrait for the class composite picture. We all went to a photograph studio for the first family photo and photos for my graduation.

After we said good-bye to Alvin, Mama and I went shopping for a formal for me to wear to the Junior-Senior banquet to be held the following week. All we could find was a peach-colored lace top gown with big puffy sleeves and a net skirt but no slip; price $9.00. I still had the pink, satin, bias-cut, night gown that had been purchased to wear under my "kitchen curtain formal" when I was a freshman.

I wore this gown to the Junior-Senior banquet. I was asked to be one of the speakers for the Junior-Senior banquet. My topic was "the rose," our class flower.

A few days before my high school graduation exercises, Mama said, "I was goin' ask Lyle to tak' you to the Senior Dance. But of course now he can't." I was shocked and surprised; I didn't understand. I had heard nothing at school about an after graduation dance. I knew if I had expressed a desire to go to a dance I would have been told, "Dancin' is a sin!" I had lost a desire to even think about attending "fun" activities for young people. Poor Mama could not realize how inappropriate it would have been for a 26 year old married man to accompany me.

Graduation day finally came! The girls wore formals and the boys wore suits. I had made a white dimity gown for graduation. What an honor it was to receive my hard earned diploma on May 19, 1943! People were shaking hands and offering congratulations after the exercises. One school board member, Mr. George Pringle, a man I hardly knew gave me the most memorable gift anyone could receive. He commented, "I think you did better than all the rest!" What a treasure to take with me forever! With God's help, I had achieved my goal of completing high school in just three years! My grade average was 93 on a three-point scale with the full 32 required credits. Was Mama proud of me? I had no idea. I do not recall any praise.

My "kitchen curtain" formal for a Valentine party

My high school graduation photo

PART IV

COLLEGE – TEACHING

SUMMER SCHOOL – 1943

Two of the three school board members of the Dixon School came to my home in April and asked me to teach their school the following year. My salary to teach five students was $100.00 a month. I signed the contract. After graduating from high school, I prepared to attend McCook Junior College at McCook, Nebraska to earn 12 hours of credit in 10 weeks to qualify to teach.

Mama surprised me with, "You'll need some new clothes; you can git a light weight coat." The Sears spring sale catalogue listed, a low priced, navy-blue coat made of casein (a milk product). I ordered it, but when it arrived, the right front side of my new navy blue coat curled inward towards the back. The lining had been cut incorrectly with the bottom of the lining too narrow for the coat. Mama added a triangle of black satin fabric to allow the front to hang properly. I wore the coat but it did not have the special feel of a new coat. My other new clothes included a pink dress, a dress made of the blue/gray/white rayon floral print, knit fabric, my graduation gift from Aunt Susan (Mama insisted I use her favorite "sack" dress style pattern), and a lavender background shell print "feed sack" dress. I had begged for a "feed sack" dress for years, which I was denied. Mama's excuse was "You are royalty. You must wear silks and satin."

McCook Junior College was located 60 miles east of Benkelman, Nebraska, a community college without dormitories. Classes began the first week of June. My parents took me to Benkelman where I boarded the Burlington train with my one cardboard suitcase.

Arrangements had been made through the College for a room at a private home. I took a taxi from the train depot to the provided downtown address. I was disappointed when I saw the tiny hot room that I was to share with another student. The furnishings included a double bed, a small dresser and a small closet for our clothes, but no study space. The landlady said, "You'll need to study at the dining room table."

I had been at the house only a few minutes when the phone rang. I had not started to unpack my suitcase. What a surprise when I was called to the phone! A friend, who I knew from Benkelman, now resided in McCook, and was calling to tell me that her landlord was looking for a young lady to baby-sit her seven-year-old daughter while the she worked the afternoon shift at the telegraph office. She asked if I would be interested. Since my classes were all in the morning, I decided I would go to meet this working mother and her daughter. I told the lady at this house about the baby-sitting job and gave up my tiny room. Then I called a taxi to go to the new house in the northwest part of town. What a contrast in the houses! This home was so large it seemed like a castle. Here I could have a nice large bed room. The mother was pleasant and the young daughter delightful. I accepted the job.

Everything went well as I settled in until bedtime. It was then that I was overtaken with the shock that **I had made a decision** to change to a different rooming house **without** Mama's approval. I cried much of that night because of fear of Mama's reactions. I was so afraid and tired of Mama's constant criticism. I wanted to please Mama as I felt I had to be perfect so she'd love me and I knew she would not be pleased with my decision. The tiny hot room at the downtown home would have been miserable. Things went better after the first night but I always feared Mama's severe ridicule. I was hoping this job would ease Mama's disapproval as now my expenses would be less. My summer school at McCook Junior College: books, tuition, and other expenses, cost less than $100.00.

Our country was involved in WWII. An army base was just outside the city limits; many army vehicles traveled past this house day and night. At the college we were told to never walk alone, even in the day time. Always have a child or another person with you. This little girl became my companion when I went shopping. I walked alone or with a classmate to and from classes in the mornings, but never alone anywhere else

Two weeks before the end of summer school, I boarded a Greyhound bus and journeyed to Beaver City, Nebraska to visit my cousin, Henry Simmons and his family on their farm. Henry was my dad's older sister's son. I had just met Henry in May at Lyle's funeral.

Saturday morning the family arose early and went to do the morning chores. I was sleeping on the couch in the living room. I had heard Henry and his sons come into the house but I did not stir. Suddenly everything was quiet, too quiet, I wondered why? Then I opened my eyes just enough for a tiny peek! **Wow**! It was a good thing I did!

Cousin Henry was standing near my head holding the cold water dipper high over my head. Behind him were his two young sons, Johnny and Phillip, each with a huge, mischievous grin on his face. "Don't you dare!" I quickly exclaimed. Results were a hardy laugh from everyone including Thelma, his wife, who quietly observed from the kitchen. When I asked, Henry what his plans were for that dipper of cold water, he never confessed but I could see a mischievous grin.

Later that day he and his family took me to visit his parents in Norton, Kansas. This was the first time I had met Aunt Alma, my dad's older sister and her husband, Melvin. It was wonderful fun filled weekend!

Finals—classes would soon end. The Public School Art class had been confusing. The instructor lectured on one aspect of art, and gave long assignments in the textbook which was difficult to understand. The surprise came with the final exam that was based entirely on that "dry" text. Everyone groaned with that realization. However, my water color drawings of pictures that depicted each of the four seasons impressed the instructor that I received a respectable passing grade. I was happy to leave the hot, hot city for the cool country farm.

SCHOOL DAYS – DIXON SCHOOL

School days at the Dixon School started in September. E.B took me to the Harry Dixon home where I would stay during the school week for the school year. Three or four weeks later he told me take the car as he did not have time to—run after me.

Mardell Dixon, Harry's younger son, one of my students, and I walked daily the mile to the school. The other family with school-aged children lived on the same road but closer to the school. Their four school-aged children joined us as we walked passed their home. My students were Raymond, grade 8, Linda and Mardell, grade 7, Harold, grade 4, and Joe, grade 2. Amy, age 5 was not old enough for grade one. Amy's mother sent her with the excuse—so she'd get used to school. I mentioned my objection about Amy to Mama but she said, "Don't say anything; show her love." The Nebraska law stated that first grade students needed to be six years old to attend school. Mama could not understand the amount of time that was required to provide special work for Amy. I needed this time to help prepare my seventh and eighth graders for the state tests.

The Dixon School was 14 miles from my home. It was a one-room school like the school I had attended except here we had a well for water. The pot-bellied stove with the stove pipe that extended over half the length of the room provided heat in the winter. I was the janitor but I had never built a fire with just kindling and coal. This often resulted in a cool, chilly room until noon.

All the school districts were short on cash from the depression. Their budgets allowed for very limited supplies. We had no library or reference books. I purchased some needed supplies and reference books from a traveling sales man. The sales man learned later that he had illegal contracts with all teachers under the age of 21. He could not collect the purchase prices of the supplies. The unique door lock was a large 10-penny nail inserted in a hole in the door frame.

The Dixon home was a two-story stucco house heated with a coal furnace in the basement with only one large vent to provide heat to the dining room and one upstairs bedroom. A coal and wood range heated the kitchen. The wind charger that set on the roof charged special batteries stored in the basement to provide electric lights, just one 40-watt bulb in each room. The parlor was heated only when they had company.

My room at the Dixon home was the large, unheated, upstairs bedroom with a large, east window. To the east of the house was the chicken house where young chickens for frying were kept. Two or three weeks after school started, the men folks talked about finding two or three dead chickens in the chicken house. The chickens were intact with just a puncture mark at the throat.

A few nights later, after I had gone to my room, I heard the usual "chattering" sounds that chickens make when they are disturbed. Immediately I went downstairs, and reported the noises. Maurice, their 21-year-old son grabbed his rifle and went to the chicken house. He saw a skunk leave the building and disappear before he could shoot it.

The next day Maurice rounded up steel traps and anchored one at each corner of the chicken house. What a surprise! The next morning a big, gorgeous, shiny, black and white skunk was in each trap. Their beautiful fur glowed in the sunlight. As Mardell and I walked to school that morning, we both expressed how we dreaded to return in the evening when the skunk odor would dominate the air.

We were surprised that evening—there was no skunk odor. Maurice said he had shot each skunk in the head before it had a chance to use nature's spray protection. Several more skunks were caught before they were all eliminated.

The last weekend of October was the annual State Teachers' Institute. All teachers were required to attend the two-day sessions at a selected location. McCook, Nebraska was the nearest location for the south-southwest area of the state. The county superintendent suggested I might be able to get a ride with three experienced teachers who were going to McCook. I was accepted for the ride. I looked forward to this training in hopes of learning new and different techniques that I could use in my classroom. My training had been limited during the ten weeks of summer school. Enroute to McCook one of the teachers carefully explained to me that they were not going to the meetings. They didn't plan to sit and listen to those "boring dumb" speakers all day. She said, "We will go, sign in, pay the dues, then leave, and go shopping. We feel the meetings are a waste of time."

I was flabbergasted! I couldn't believe what I heard. I thought, "You are showing me how you cheat. You are paid to attend these training meetings instead you choose to shop, something you should do on your own time." I never attended Institute with those teachers again.

When I went home on weekends, Mama continued to complain to me about her health problems and how hard it was for her to keep up with her work. She stated that the hemorrhage problem she had had for months was growing worse. She kept in touch with the Reverend Casebeer in New York State asking him to pray for the "spirit doctors" to heal her. A generous donation accompanied her requests.

Mama and I shared the same day bed. At night I could feel her body wrench and jerk each night immediately after we went to bed. She would say, "The "spirit doctors" are healing me. They will heal me like the woman who touched Jesus' garment hem." The hemorrhaging grew worse while Mama faithfully followed the Reverend Casebeer's recommendations except now she called him "Dr. Casebeer." She even packed herself with cotton and vinegar as he had recommended still the hemorrhaging continued. She grew weaker. The clotting and hemorrhaging finally became so bad that Mama became afraid. It was then she asked my dad to go to Uncle Andy's and call for the doctor at Imperial, Nebraska to come.

Imperial had a small hospital but the only doctor was on call for the night and could not leave for a house call. Uncle Andy had a telephone exchange—this meant that calls could be made to either Imperial or Benkelman from his house (At that time each county had its own telephone exchange system). Dr. Moorehouse, the new doctor in Benkelman, was called. He had built the first small hospital for Benkelman in 1941, just three years after his arrival. His station wagon was equipped with a small stretcher, so he could transport patients to the hospital. He came immediately. Mama was so weak that she had to be lifted from her bed onto the stretcher in the house and carried to the doctor's car. He left promptly for the hospital in Benkelman. Mama needed treatment that was not available at Dr. Moorehouse's small hospital. He immediately arranged for her to go to St. Luke's Hospital in Denver, Colorado, which was over 200 miles away.

With permission from my school board, I left school to go with Mama to St. Luke's Hospital in Denver for treatments. I rode in the "ambulance" which was actually a funeral hearse. As the vehicle traveled through Wray, Colorado, a dip in the road caused the driver to swerve. I was thrown out of my seat where I sat in the back beside Mama. I received a severe bump on the head. The driver stopped and insisted that I sit in the front passenger seat while the driver's assistant rode in the back beside Mama's stretcher.

At the hospital I was referred to a rooming house across the street from the hospital. Mama was comfortable now. I had never been around any serious illness and was bored, as I always had to be working at home.

It was December, and a two inch snow had fallen during the night. I had not taken my overshoes. I visited the Denver Zoo, Museum of Natural History; and a girl friend from the Rollwitz Youth group who attended Colorado State College in Denver. Later I toured the State House; here I became confused with all four exits looking the same from the inside. With all of my walking, my shoes became saturated with the melting snow.

I could not sit around. The next afternoon I filled water pitchers at the hospital as patients were begging for water but was told that I could not do that without applying for a job. The head nurse had been so rude to me that I looked for work elsewhere.

I applied for a job at a Brecht Candy factory in downtown Denver. I was hired and immediately went to work hand-packing chocolates. I had not brought a lunch with me as I had not expected to go to work immediately. At noon two older ladies accompanied me to the nearest restaurant which was a saloon. I was only 18, an illegal customer. I ordered a hamburger sandwich that was the most horrible, tasting hamburger I had ever eaten. It tasted spoiled. After that, I took my lunch. After work I'd go to the hospital and see Mama. The altitude and I were not compatible. Malts were my main diet at 15 or 25 cents each, which was very economical.

The fourth day at work I was feeling badly. I stopped to visit Mama and was in her room when her nurse came in. Mama mentioned that I was feeling poorly. The nurse felt my forehead, and immediately sent me away because I had a fever. Mama's doctor came to my room the next day and diagnosed my problem—flu. As soon as I was feeling better, I went home to teach. Mama seemed to be getting along fine. I was never told anything about her treatments or the diagnosis. I returned home on the Greyhound bus. I had missed more than a week of teaching.

I taught school just two days when Dr. Moorehouse phoned the Dixon home. He said that the Denver doctors thought Mama might have cancer. Surgery was mentioned and that frightened me. I knew Mama would not agree to surgery. I left the next day on the Burlington train. When I returned, the hospital staff was not happy as I was just 18, a minor, and no one would talk to me about Mama. They had wanted my dad to come. If he had gone, he would not have been helpful. My parents had limited association with any of the neighbors. No one would have been available to care for the livestock. I could not take care of the animals, morning and night and drive back and forth to school each day.

When I returned to Denver, I was determined to stay until Mama was dismissed. She was very weak. She had to travel home by ambulance. I accompanied her to the local hospital where she spent a few days before she returned to the farm. She frequently remarked that she had a burned spot on her back that had been caused by the x-ray. I was unaware that x-ray was used to treat cancer at that time. I never knew what her treatments were for as the only thing she ever referred to was a fibroid tumor. She did not seem to know much about her illness. It took months for her to regain her strength. I went back to teaching. I had missed over two weeks of school. This meant that the end of school would be delayed until later in April.

My first trip home from Denver was on a Greyhound Bus. When the bus made the rest stop in Wray, Colorado, I shopped for a small Christmas tree, and some decorations to use at my school.

After school closed for Christmas vacation, I brought my little tree home still in the stand without the decorations. I took it into the house and set it on the little table in the corner of the kitchen-dining-family room. Mama made sure I was so busy that I never had time to replace any of the decorations. I was disgusted. Mama never said anything but I imagine it was a sin to have a Christmas tree.

When Mama saw the moss green umbrella skirt that I had purchased with my teaching money, she said, "You can call that umbrella skirt my Christmas present to you."

"Why," I silently protested, "You have never given me a Christmas present before. Why now?" I could never feel that skirt was a gift from her since I earned the money to purchase it. I wondered, "Does Mama believe that my wages belong to her?"

WINTER – SPRING – 1944

During the second week of January, 1944, a severe blizzard struck western Nebraska. Mama's orders were that during bitter cold temperature the battery had to be removed from the car and kept inside the house to prevent it from freezing. The Dixon men questioned this practice but assisted me.

Every day after the blizzard, Mardell and I walked to school on top of the three and four-foot wind sculptured ice-encrusted snowdrifts. After a month, some of the roads had been opened. With help from Mardell and Maurice, I put chains on the rear wheels of the car to provide traction in the snow. I drove to school that Friday morning and planned to start home immediately after school, and left as planned. I had driven over to and onto Highway 61 to the "cut-across road" that normally saved me eight miles of travel. Suddenly I realized a team and wagon was nearby on the cut-across road. Mardell and Maurice had driven a team and wagon through belly deep, snow drifts to stop me from continuing towards home. A telephone message had come to the Dixon home saying that the roads were not passable from Benkelman out to the farm. My dad, at Mama's request, had to have driven a team and wagon to the Lutz home the nearest telephone to make the call.

I returned to the Dixon home. Immediately Mrs. Dixon announced that she and Mr. Dixon were leaving to attend the Farm Bureau meeting in Benkelman. Fear engulfed me, as I was afraid to stay in the house with Mardell and his older brother, Maurice. She went on to say, "You can prepare oyster soup for your supper. The oysters are in the refrigerator. Maurice can get the milk from the back porch." Then they were gone.

I was stunned. I had done baking but Mama always did the cooking. "What am I to do?" I silently questioned. I was so accustomed to hiding my feelings. I tried to act knowledgeable of the task at hand. With trembling hands, I found a saucepan, and added the oysters. I do not recall if I cooked the oysters before I added the milk or not. Maurice had brought the milk into the kitchen from the back porch as his mother had asked. I added the milk to the oysters and seasoned the soup with a little salt and pepper. Mardell set bowels, spoons and crackers on the dining room table.

I placed the saucepan of hot oyster soup with a soup ladle on a hot pad on the table. We sat down to eat. Maurice took only a few sips of the soup from his bowl, then got up from the table said, "I'm going to Frazier's." I knew his girl friend was one of the Frazier girls, yet I wondered why he left so abruptly without eating his bowl of soup. I tasted the soup and thought, "What is that 'peculiar tangy taste?'" as I consumed my soup. Mardell ate a little of the soup then popped a big bowl of popcorn. I stored the leftover soup in the kerosene-powered refrigerator.

The next day my puzzle about limited consumption of the oyster soup was solved when Mrs. Dixon said, "I told Maurice to get the sweet milk setting at the south end of the table, but he got the buttermilk from the north end of the table." I immediately knew why the oyster soup had a "peculiar tangy flavor." I never confessed that was the first time I had prepared oyster soup.

Two weeks later, I again started for home. I left school at 4 p.m. and drove to Benkelman. Then I began my search for roads north and west to my parent's farm. During my travels that night I drove through barnyards, front yards, backyards, over barbed wire fences anchored on the ground, and through fields, anywhere a trail had been blazed between or around snowdrifts.

Finally, after more than four hours of driving more than 30 miles, I arrived at the Frank Graham home about 8 p.m. It was dark and I was still a mile from home. I stopped to inquire about the road condition at the sandy twin hills. "It's not good as it is badly drifted. You'd be safer to spend the night. In the morning you can see the wheel tracks better." Frank stated caringly. I stayed and left after daylight the next morning. I finally made it home around 10 a.m. It had taken me over 16 hours to travel the 14 miles from the Dixon school to my home.

Several times during the school year, I took the road that trailed past Uncle Andy's home. They lived four miles from my home. I'd stop and visit with them briefly, but I never shared that news with Mama as she did want me to visit them.

The rest of the eight-month school year was uneventful. About a week before school was to be out in April, Vera, my brother, Alvin's wife, who had been visiting for several weeks with her family in Benkelman, stopped for a visit. She told of her plans to return to their home in Downey, California with their two pre-school aged children. She asked me to take them to Ogallala, Nebraska to catch the Union Pacific train to California. The day she planned to leave was just one day before my last day of school. I begged, "Please wait one more day, then I could accompany you, and help with the children." But she insisted on leaving as planned. That day the roads were wet and slippery from a light spring snow that covered the icy, frozen ruts. It was a long tiring one-way 100 mile trip to Ogallala. I had longed to visit my brother in California, but like my dad, I still haven't made it to California.

SUMMER SCHOOL –
HASTINGS COLLEGE

June 1944 arrived and I was off to summer school again. I did not enjoy attending McCook Junior College and living in private a home. I wanted to live on campus in a dormitory. I selected Hastings College at Hastings, Nebraska, which was sponsored by the Presbyterian Church. Mama had kept telling me how to teach and what I could or could not do, so I decided then and there, no more classes towards a teaching license. She also told me that she expected me to be the county school superintendent. I wondered—if she knew that was a political position. Politics were not for me.

I enjoyed singing and considered that to be an interesting career. I did not realize I needed an extensive musical background or that I would need an accompanist. I had taught myself to read notes for the melody and play our foot-pedal, pump parlor organ. I had begged to take piano lessons. We talked with a piano teacher in Benkelman, who said, "You can practice on your organ and recite on my piano." I tried that once and explained to the teacher that the piano and organ needed completely different touch. I would not do that. I had my brother, Lyle's violin. I tried violin lessons by correspondence, but that was a joke. I even borrowed a steel guitar, but without an instructor that was not helpful. I played sacred and old-time songs on the organ by ear, and the harmonica. I loved to sing along with the records on our wind-up phonograph.

My first experiences with voice lessons were very disappointing. The instructor showed little interest in teaching as she would be late. She suggested

I press a buzzer to call her in her apartment above the studio. When I did, she was unhappy.

I enjoyed living in a dorm. My roommate, Doris was enrolled in the large Cadet Nursing Corp. classes. Nurses were desperately needed during WWII. The government provided free three-year training for the young ladies. After graduation, the nurses would be assigned to work for the government at selected area hospitals for three years to repay for the training.

Doris and her friend, Jane, also a Cadet Nurse, and I enjoyed shopping and entertainment off campus in Hastings. Ladies were never to go off campus alone, because a training base for soldiers and sailors was nearby. I enjoyed having a roommate and other dorm friends.

I was surprised to learn this church sponsored college allowed smoking. After I had read literature from Aunt Susan, a Seventh Day Adventist, that stated smoking could harm our bodies which were Christ's temple, I had rejected smoking. Also, when I was in the fifth grade, my one-room grade school teacher brought to school a white handkerchief that showed the black residue deposited on it as her brother drew the smoke from the cigarette into his lungs. That was definitely not appealing to me.

Earlier that spring my parents, who never smoked tobacco cigarettes, began smoking Dr. R. Schiffmann's Asthmador Herbal Cigarettes. These cigarettes were advertised as an herbal treatment for asthma. My dad suffered with asthma. Mama told me they would not hurt me because they are made with herbs and mullein. That sounded like permission for me to smoke.

I recalled when I was nine; she had given me a regular cigarette that she had taken from Alvin. After she took a puff, she gave it to me. "Com' on, it won't hurt you," I heard both Mama and Alvin, encouraged, "Take a deep breath." I obeyed, as I was always required to do. After that one puff! I was so sick! My head spun around and my eyes—I was so sick! Mama and Alvin both laughed at me which infuriated me. I never understood their actions.

I tried the herbal cigarettes, as smoking was very socially acceptable. I smoked one or two a day for a few days, and then I began to crave them. I tossed that package like a whizzing bullet into the nearest trash can! It was months before the craving diminished.

I was dismayed when the summer dorm party was held and we were told each of us had to have a date. I had met Jim, a pianist, in the music practice building. He was one of the few male students on campus. He accompanied Jean, a lady singer. I had assumed they dated as I saw them together daily. I wanted to ask Jim but felt I would be intruding. At the party Jim accompanied

Jean for a solo, then left. Then I knew that she had another steady boy friend, but it was too late to ask Jim.

Many of the ladies dated servicemen from the base, and had invited them to the party. Both soldiers and sailors were at the Hastings base. I finally agreed for another gal to ask a soldier to be my date. When the soldiers arrived, no one introduced me. I was in the dorm's parlor where others met their dates. I became so discouraged. I violated the rule that no one was to be in her second floor room as each room was to be empty and the door locked. The downstairs room doors had to be open at all times. I went upstairs to my room and locked my door. I don't think I was ever missed.

Later I learned Aunt Lulu lived just four miles from Hastings. I had never met Aunt Lulu, my dad's younger sister. Had I known she lived nearby, I would have had a wonderful weekend with her. Mama never wanted me to get acquainted with any of my dad's family.

The presence of the servicemen kept the war in everyone's mind. There was also an ammunition dump nearby where explosives were made for the war. The weirdest thing was seeing people who worked in the manufacturing of these ammunitions. Their skin, white of their eyes, their hair, and finger nails had all turned a yellowish green. Later I learned that the chemical was nitroglycerin which left the people who worked with these explosives with many adverse health affects

During the third week of July, Mama's letter stated that Alvin had telegraphed her that her father, Mike Grams a California resident, had suddenly passed away. Alvin had wanted Mama to come to the funeral. Mama indicated that she was interested in going. I dutifully talked to my instructors and officials at the college saying that Mama needed me to accompany her to the funeral. I was allowed to skip the last week of summer school with full credits. But when I arrived home, Mama denied she had expressed a desire to attend the funeral. I was disappointed again.

During August I planned to redesign my blue/gray/white floral print, jersey knit dress that Mama had insisted I had to make in the sack dress style. I had worn this dress one Sunday morning to church. One of the ladies in the church choir, that I had joined, made a casual remark about the style of my dress. She wasn't rude, but I'd heard so many rude remarks about my clothes for years that I could not wear that dress again.

To redesign the dress, I placed it on the ironing board and measured down the underarm seam on each side about seven inches and marked each spot with a pin. I began to cut across the dress from pin to pin. Too late, Mama saw that I had cut my nice jersey dress into two pieces. "If I had known what you were going to do, I would have stopped you," she stated with a raw tone.

"I'm redesigning this dress." I calmly replied. After I had cut the dress into two pieces, I ripped the matching skirt that was made from the left over pieces. I added a set-in belt to the bodice, sewed the rest of the skirt fabric from the dress and the fabric from the separate skirt together, and pleated it. Then I attached it to the set-in belt. It was an attractive dress that I loved to wear.

SCHOOL NORTH OF MAX, NEBRASKA

In early August, two school board members of a school north of Max, Nebraska, came to my home in search of a teacher for 12 students in grades one through eight. One of these men was the school treasurer. One of my stipulations was that I needed a room in which to stay, not far from the school, for the winter months. I wanted to avoid driving on 35 miles of rural roads, which could be very treacherous in the winter snow. The treasurer agreed that I could depend on a room at his home. He lived a quarter of mile from the school. The other board member stated that Mrs. Barns who lived about a mile from the school often kept the teacher until her father came to stay during the coldest weather. These arrangements sounded acceptable but nothing was put in writing. I signed the teaching contract; classes started the first Monday of September.

I planned to live at home while Alvin was home doing the fall farm work in preparation to take over the farm operations. (He had lived in California during the war and planned to return to farm in Nebraska. He had signed an agreement with my parents to operate the farm.) Alvin had quit his job as a welder at the Long Beach shipyards where he had repaired Navy ships during the war. His wife, Vera and their children were to remain in California until their home was sold. I had seen my big brother only a few times in my life that I wanted to get to know him better. I drove daily to school while he was at the farm.

Corn husking had just begun when I picked up my September check. The school treasurer said, "Must be nice to sit behind a desk and get paid to do nothing."

His words angered me. I calmly challenged him with, "I will be glad to husk corn for you for a day while you sit behind my desk and teach if you think it is so easy. I have husked corn and would have no problem." He never accepted my challenge, but I suspected he did not like teachers.

This was another community without a house of worship. After I obtained permission from the school board to use the school on Sunday mornings for Sunday school, I asked the Reverend Jones, the missionary minister of the American Sunday School Union, to organize Sunday school services. Mama accompanied me for two or three Sundays. I led the singing without piano or organ. It was the same old thing with Mama. This time she said, "You sing too loudly when you lead the singin.'"

My ego was crushed again. I thought – aren't song leaders to sing out so they can be heard. In my observations that had been true. I relayed my observations to her. She rarely left the farm to go anywhere. I wondered how could she know what was the proper thing to do? "Why are you always criticizing me?" My inner person silently protested. "Do you hate me that much?"

Early in December, a blizzard made the roads nearly impassable. Now was time for me to change my room to the home of the treasurer. I was disappointed when he said, "We don't want our little daughter to have to give up her room." The treasurer knew of his three-year old daughter's needs when he promised me a room. I felt betrayed.

I had to drive the 35 miles on snow-choked roads daily to get to school. I thought I had avoided this dilemma when I requested arrangements before I signed the contact. Finally one of the mothers, Mrs. Rhodes, who had three children in school said, "You can stay at our house. We don't have an extra room but there is an extra bed in our daughters' room that you may use." To show my appreciation, I accepted her offer. They were a very nice family and the children were well behaved, but I just could not relax sharing a room with two of my pupils. The children and I walked over a mile in the snow to school. I stayed with this family until Christmas vacation.

Our Christmas gift exchange and party was Friday, a few days before Christmas. The school board treasurer brought my check to the school. I suggested an adjustment of the number of days for Christmas vacation, and stated my concern that blizzards could block the roads so I could not get to school at all. I do not recall the vacation time noted in my contract. Immediately the treasurer said, "No, that is not acceptable," and indicated I could drive. To me that was not acceptable.

I felt the school board treasurer had not been fair with me. I said, "I was promised a room near the school before I signed that contract. Now there is no guarantee that I will be able to get to school." He suggested that

I could resign. I felt I could no longer trust the school board treasurer. Sadly I resigned.

When Mama learned of the incident, **fire flew**! "You are the most terrible person! They can't do that to you and I'm goin' see that you git back to teachin' that school," she exploded. I explained to her that the treasurer had not kept his agreement and I felt I had no choice. I did not realize it at that moment, that Mama's belief "I should not rock the boat but accept what others demanded, regardless, in other words – **be a door mat** – was not followed when I resigned.

On Monday of the following week, she accompanied me to make sure I did what she demanded. First, we went to the county school superintendent, Mrs. Logan, who stated she had heard from the school board, and they were uncertain about the future. Teachers were scarce. Then Mama insisted I go back to the school board. I felt like a big fool but what choice did I have except to obey. A nineteen-year old was a minor and had no rights but obey her parents. A minor could not rent an apartment, only room with a family. Mama did the talking but she learned that there was to be no reversal of things. I would not have felt comfortable going back to teach in that school anyway.

Again I heard what a "terrible person I was." Those thoughts remained on Mama's mind the rest of her life. Over the years she had frequently reminded me of this incident with "you are a terrible person." Fact is those were the last words she spoke to me. In 1982, while I sat in a chair at the foot of Mama's bed in the nursing home in Benkelman, Nebraska where she had resided the previous three months. She repeated those words again. I said, "Mom, I do not have to listen to that any more." I got up, said, "Good bye," kissed her on the forehead and left. I told the nursing staff why I was leaving. The staff said that Mama was quiet when I was absent, but her behavior was completely changed when I was present. She was always asking me to sue someone.

Tears accompanied me that night after I left the nursing home as I drove my friend, Wynona's car to her home in Benkelman. Wynona was a wonderful friend – she let me stay with her and use her car as I needed. She was a granddaughter of Teresa Shrum, the homestead widow, who had given Mama a home many years before.

I had traveled over 1,000 miles to be with Mama, but I could no longer tolerate her humiliating hateful words. She had pushed me away once too often. I left Benkelman, Nebraska for my home in New Castle, Indiana on the bus the next morning. Mama passed away three days later. I returned to Nebraska to complete arrangements for her funeral.

As the only surviving child, I asked to read her will after I had completed funeral arrangements. Miss Owens, Mama's attorney, gave me the understanding that I could not do that for five months. That did not sound right to me so I spoke to Mr. Drulinger, my attorney who said "You have the right to read that will now. Tell Miss Owens to deliver it to the judge's office."

I called Miss Owens back and said, "I understand that I have the right to read Mama's will now." She asked where I got that information. I needed only to say, "My attorney . . . ." Immediately she said that her secretary would have the will at the County Judge's office in 20 minutes. I went to the County Judge's office. Tears flowed down my cheeks as I sat reading the beginning words to the will: "To my beloved daughter. . . ."

Mama's words from the past have haunted me for years "You are a terrible person". When I think of all the negatives like: vermifuge daily (Ugh! What a taste!) for years because I gritted my teeth at night as a toddler; punishment when I was injured at school; the enemas several times a week during grade school years with lye soap suds to "kill all the germs;" required to wear that bag of stinky old asafetida plus eating raw garlic just before going to school; and refused to let me speak to my class mates when we met in town. She always told me I was "a terrible person," so terrible that when I called her on the phone from my home in Indiana during 1970's that she said, "You need to get down on your knees and pray," then hung up. She said, "Don't ever to trust my grandchildren," and she even accused Edna, her niece, of throwing a "fire bomb" against her house. Plus, the last time my husband, two teenage daughters and I visited Mama, she accused us of stealing the slats from the bed my husband and I slept in

"Mama," I wondered –"Were you mixed up? Or depressed or what? Or were you trying to protect me from some imagined horrid happening like you had experienced at the hands of men? Or did you have one of your "visions" that told you about the "future?" Or had you been referring to something you gleaned on your Ouija board? Or were you just trying to protect me from life? Why? Why?" I will never know.

STERLING COLLEGE – 1945

Immediately after January 1, I started making plans to attend college. Arkilee, one of the members of the Rollwitz Youth Group, had been attending Sterling

College at Sterling, Kansas .and highly recommended this college sponsored by the United Presbyterian Church. Arkilee related that the popular social activities such as smoking, drinking, and dancing were not allowed on campus. I was very drawn to Sterling as a Christian school since few social activities had been part of my life.

I applied and was delighted to be accepted. Among the limited items I would need was an electric desk lamp, I wrote saying, "We don't have electricity. I've no desk lamp." Their reply encouraged me to come with, "We'll work something out." However I was able to find a brown, gooseneck, desk lamp before I left for college.

We had gone to Benkelman, Nebraska to sell the eggs and cream. I had my two cardboard suitcases in the car, and I expected to be taken to the Greyhound Bus station in Bird City, Kansas. While we were in the Campbell Produce Store, Mama stunned me with, "The tires on the car aren't good enough to take you the 25 miles to meet the bus at Bird City, Kansas. You will have to find your own way there." She had not given a hint about the "bad" tires when I protested driving 35 miles twice daily on drifted roads to teach at the school north of Max, Nebraska. Tires and gas were still on the ration list. Farmers could get a supply of gas easier than tires. The only tires available were used recapped tires that were not dependable.

God was with me—a man and a woman—who we did not know had overheard Mama's remark and my protest. Immediately the woman spoke up, "We live near Bird City and we will be happy to give you a ride to the Greyhound bus station." I never knew their names but thanked them. I really believe this was another way Mama was trying to impress her authority on me that I had to do as she said. She frequently told me to get a good education and make "something of yourself," then denied me the opportunity.

Sterling College was wonderful. I was treated with respect, which was a new experience for me. I tried to be polite and respectful but I am sure my discomfort showed. Even saying "Thank You" was difficult.

The campus was small with just four buildings: Spencer Hall housed the administration offices, auditorium, and music practice rooms; Wilson Gym was for sports for men with a recreation room for all students; Campbell Hall was the women's dormitory with a sleeping porch on the third floor; and Cooper Hall, the original building, provided the classrooms and the school library. A small power plant, set across the back alley near the football field provided steam heat. The cafeteria was in the basement of Campbell Hall. Men stayed in private homes.

With a student body of around 100 students, it was possible to know everyone on campus. I thoroughly enjoyed being a student at Sterling. Attendance at chapel on Wednesday mornings was a requirement as well as church attendance on Sunday. There were four churches in Sterling: United Presbyterian, Methodist, Baptist, and Reformed Presbyterian. I, like many of the students, visited all of the churches.

Sterling College was a well known pre-ministerial college. Over eighty percent of the students were planning to attend seminary or go into missionary work. Sterling, also, had an outstanding musical program.

I was able to find part-time work on campus. The cafeteria needed many part-time students to assist in preparing foods, and washing dishes and the dreaded pots and pans. I spent many hours working in the cafeteria. There were very few restaurants in Sterling. Sunday noon dinner in the college cafeteria was a way the community constantly supported the college. Sterling was a small college town in central Kansas.

I was a second semester freshman and needed just two hours credit to be qualified as a sophomore. During the winter months, while I was teaching, I took correspondence courses from the University of Nebraska to add to my college credits. I continued my focus in music but soon learned that this field was not within my financial means or background experience.

I met another second semester student, Joyce from Hammond, Indiana. Joyce and I shared several classes. We became good friends and attended the Baptist Church with Dorothy and Lila, sisters who were from Wallace, Kansas. The four of us had many happy times together.

I had attended the Baptist Church regularly with Joyce, Lila and Dorothy, and sang in the church choir. We attended mid-week prayer meetings. I seriously considered joining the church but after reading a little information booklet on the church beliefs provided by the pastor, I changed my mind. The pastor, also a Sterling student, was unhappy when I said I would not be joining his church. In that information booklet, I learned that my name had to be on their church role to partake of communion. No one had ever discussed communion or baptism with me, but my personal feelings were that I would not join a church that prohibited believers from partaking of communion unless their name was on that church's roll book. I knew baptism would be by immersion. I began to explore the church rules of the United Presbyterian Church and learned that communion was open to all believers. The United Presbyterian Church accepted all forms of baptism which agreed with my personal belief.

I joined the United Presbyterian Church on March 22, 1945 with baptism at the Baptist Church on April 1, 1945. The Reverend M.N. Nichol officiated. Both the Baptist minister and Mama were displeased with my decision. She said I was deserting the Rollwitz Church. She could not realize that there was no church at Rollwitz, just a Sunday school and a youth group with a semi-retired minister to provide a sermon once a month. Mama had often talked about big Sunday School Conferences of the past as if she had been actively involved. This I could never picture.

I took my first sewing class during this semester. I was so nervous using a pattern that my hand shook as I cut around the pattern pieces. I chose a simple cotton dress. When Miss Oline, the Home Economics Professor, graded my finished garment, she found gathers that I had overlooked where I had accidentally caught the shoulder with gathers as I gathered the sleeve. I was so embarrassed when she said, "We only gather the sleeve, not the shoulder." It was then I realized that I had not checked my garment thoroughly before turning it in for a grade. This class was the turning point in my search for a major. I focused on home economics classes, which I thoroughly enjoyed. I continued to include Bible, English, and science. Biology was fascinating, as was astronomy.

I met Dorothy and her sister, Ellen, from Hutchinson, Kansas. Dorothy was Director of the Business Office; Ellen was a freshman in the education program. Dorothy invited me to their home in Hutchinson many times for fun activities during my time in Sterling.

SUMMER SCHOOL – 1945

During the summer the students planned their own recreation activities. Softball was a favorite activity. One week the group went to Lyons, Kansas about 10 miles away for a swim party at the closest swimming pool to Sterling. Swimming was a wonderful relief from the hot Kansas summer. I loved swimming but a few days after this swimming party, I began having a sore throat, a very severe sore throat. A trip to the Sterling Clinic gave me the diagnosis: strep throat. I received a prescription for the new sulfa drug, developed during WWII. It had to be taken with baking soda. To this day, I can hardly eat food prepared with baking soda. I was unable to attend classes, which resulted in an incomplete for one class.

After summer school ended, the dorm closed; I had to leave. Having no way to contact my parents except by mail, I prepared to travel home by bus when I should not have been traveling. The fever was gone but I was very weak.

Alvin and his family had moved into the three-roomed farmhouse with my parents. He and his family occupied the front room. They met me at the bus station in Bird City, Kansas. With the car windows down, I could not get out of the draft caused by the wind blowing through the car. I had a set-back in my recovery which took weeks to overcome.

I had planned to return to classes at Sterling College in the fall. But Mama with her "school-needs-a-teacher-oriented-antenna" focused and learned that the Champion High School needed a teacher or it would be closed. She wanted me to take the special test and teach at the school. I took the test, but was told that my math score was not high enough to receive a temporary certificate to teach high school. It was a blessing, as teaching high school students was not included in my grade school training. (Again something Mama could not understand.) However, a one-room grade school about six miles south of Champion needed a teacher. I applied and was accepted. Before I signed the contract, the school board stated that they had no money to pay a teacher. Instead of a check, I would receive a voucher which could I cash at the bank, or keep it until the fall taxes were collected, then cash it and receive the interest.

Since I would not be returning to Sterling College for the fall semester, I had to make a trip over 350 miles each way to college to complete my summer school classes. During my absence, Mama told Alvin to move his family out of the house. It was then he learned that the new house that he had requested in the signed contract to take over the farm operation would never be built. He rented a house in Benkelman where his daughter started first grade.

SCHOOL DISTRICT 14, CHASE COUNTY, NEBRASKA

District #14 in Chase County, a one-room school, was about six miles south of Champion, Nebraska, and over 30 miles from my home. The roads to my home were tire tracks, originally wagon trails, worn in the sandy soil of the prairie. The pastures on each side of the road were marked with barbed wire fences. If vehicles approached from each direction, each vehicle would give one tire track until they passed.

Rural Electrification had reached this part of Chase County, but District #14 had no funds to connect to the electrical line that passed the school. My eight students were in grades one, two, four and five.

Halloween was a time for a big celebration. The students prepared a program of readings, skits and songs. The parents brought kerosene lanterns and Aladdin gas lights for illumination. A special treat—the school had a foot-pump parlor organ. I played the melody of the songs with my right hand. After the program, we "halloweened" the room with corn stalks, and made a real mess of things before we went home.

The next school day, the students and I put the room in order before classes. The students had as much fun with the cleanup as in the Halloween activities.

Several times the students asked when my boy friend was coming to school. "I don't have a boyfriend." I replied. They told me about a former teacher's boy friend who came often. Teacher and her boy friend would sit at the back of the room and kiss and kiss. "We had fun watching them even though we were supposed to be studying," they confessed and laughed.

I stayed a few weeks with Gertrude, a Catholic lady. She and I had serious talks about religion and church rules. I did not pry but was glad she was very willing to share about the Catholic faith, which we discussed. Mama was fiercely against Catholics. Later I learned that the string of blue glass beads assembled with metal chain between the beads and with a cross (crucifix) that I had played with as a child was a rosary. The little red prayer book that I had read prayers from for grace before meals was a Catholic prayer book. Then I wondered where Mama had obtained these items of Catholic worship.

Finally, through my genealogy research, I was able to have an old letter written in old German translated. In that letter it was noted that Mama's first stepmother, Fredericka Keyser was Catholic. Fredericka was the woman who insisted that her new American husband, Mike Grams, my grandpa, kick out his young daughter, my mama, so Fredericka's two children could reside with them.

After Gertrude left to spend the winter with a relative, I changed my residence to the home of Eldon, one of my students. He and I walked the mile to school together.

His older sister, Charlene, attended Beauty School in Denver, Colorado. She came home with her soldier husband the last day of school before

Christmas vacation. A blizzard late in the week had created unsafe traveling conditions for me to travel in the dark over the tire trail roads. I spent Friday night with the family. Isla, the younger sister, gave her bedroom to her sister, Charlene and her husband. Isla and I shared my bed that night.

A big party was given on that Friday night, celebrating Charlene's marriage and homecoming. The guests smoked cigars until the air was clouded with the second-hand smoke. This family did not smoke. The second-hand smoke penetrated every room in the house and gave me a headache. I could hardly sleep due to lack of fresh air. I was happy to leave the next morning.

In November, Floy asked me to prepare a Christmas program for the Rollwitz Church. Arkilee, Floy's daughter, returned from Sterling College for her Christmas vacation after I had the program planned, rehearsed and nearly ready for presentation. Arkilee wanted to take over the program. "No," I said, "I was asked to plan the program. It will be presented as planned." Arkilee, a pianist, felt she should have that honor. I was so nervous during the program presentation that I perspired until my dress was wet from under my arm pits to my waistline

WINTER – SPRING – 1946

My students and I returned to school after Christmas vacation with the usual snow and cold weather. Everyone loved to play the game of "Fox and Geese." When enough snow was on the ground, we walked to form a large apple-pie circle then cut across the circle like cutting a pie with our footsteps. When we wanted a more challenging game, a smaller circle would be stepped off inside the larger circle. One child would be the "fox"– his den was the center where the "cuts" crossed. The object was to catch the "geese"—all the other children, until all were taken to "fox's den."

In fifth grade arithmetic, long division was problematic for one student. Her papers were very neat with all answers correct. I said, "Would you show all the steps you used to solve these problems? Show all the work on your paper."

The next day her very neat paper showed all the steps used to solve the problems. I was curious because her paper seemed too neat. I asked her and my other fifth grade student to work a problem on the board and show all the steps to solve the problem. She was stuck; she had no idea how to solve the problem. From that day on, she was not allowed to take her arithmetic book home. She had had too much help from home plus her book had the answers in the back, which was not unusual at that time.

About six weeks before the end of school, I was walking around the classroom observing my students at work. I hesitated a moment at one fifth grade student's desk. She looked at me with fire in her eyes and hate in her voice as she vehemently said, "I hate you!" The shock of hearing those words automatically brought my hand up for a slap on her face. I was aghast! I did not hate her. I wondered what had I done to cause her to feel that way? I could not understand her words or my instant inappropriate reaction to them. Since that happening, I have tried to understand my instant reaction. I have thought—could it have been because I had heard so many undertones of hate from my parents?

I shook so much inside that I could hardly walk or talk. I was nauseated. I had objected to her spitting the greenish phlegm she coughed up on the school ground. "I have chronic bronchitis," she replied, but I did not make a big issue of that very bad habit.

This fifth-grader and her second-grade brother never returned to school. I was not sure if I had a job any more, but the school board said, "We are behind you." That statement made me feel that was a girl with a problem in the past. I resolved that this would be my last year teaching. My teaching certificate would expire at the end of the school year anyway.

In April while still teaching, Mama demanded that the field work needed to be done **now.** My dad was not getting it done as fast as she had demanded. She said, "You can use the tractor and disc to chop the corn stalks before and after school hours." This was unusual as a disc was rarely used in our sandy soil because the loose soil would drift more on windy days. Now I was getting out into the field around 5:00 a.m., chopping corn stalks until around 7:30 coming in with the tractor, washing up, and changing clothes then driving the 30 miles to school. Immediately after school I had to leave for home and get out into the field until dark. There was no time or energy for lesson planning, or grading papers. I was exhausted and relieved when school was out. I commented about pay for this extra hard work but Mama just indicated, "You will get tuition money."

* * *

One Saturday in June, I had motored to Parks, Nebraska to deliver eggs to the Kulhman's Grocery Store and ship two five-gallon cans of cream to the Creamery at Hastings, Nebraska. As I breezed along towards home on the graded dirt road, I saw a large ditch had been washed out across the road just pass the Pflum farm house. I stopped to allow the oncoming vehicle to pass.

When I tried to shift from high into low, I was astonished to see the stick gear-shifter of the 1933 V-8 Ford was in my hand unattached to the transmission. Panic and fear set in: What have I done now? What am I going to do? I was so afraid of Mama. Now she would blame me for damaging the family car. I had asked to buy my own car, but she said, "You have a car to use; you don't need to buy one." A woman could not go to an automobile dealer and buy a car – a man had to sign the note. Women were still considered incapable of managing money, and as a minor, I had no legal rights.

Calmly I sized up the shifter in my hand. I was puzzled—what should I do? I wondered if I slipped this shifter back into the transmission, would it work? That was my only choice. Sure enough it fit into place perfectly and the gears meshed with perfection. Immediately, I was on my way home. That shifter lifted out of its place several more times while I drove the car.

SUMMER SCHOOL – 1946

I returned to Sterling for my second summer session. The previous summer I had taken my first sewing class. I loved sewing and Miss Oline was an excellent instructor. This summer in clothing class I made a tangerine floral print dressy dress. I loved sewing and preferred using a pattern, now that I understood the directions.

Bicycles were the chosen campus vehicle. Students would whiz to classes and downtown. I had always wanted a bicycle, but Mama said it would not be usable in our sandy yard. My pastor, The Reverend M. N. Nichol, his wife, and their two children each had a bicycle instead of a family car. I asked Mrs. Nichol, "May I borrow your bicycle to learn to ride?" She consented. I am not sure she realized I'd never ridden a bicycle. I borrowed her bike three times. As I was nearing the parsonage to return the bike, after my third practice session, it seemed to have a mind of its own; I tried to keep it on the sidewalk. Instead we were headed straight for the big oak tree in front of the parsonage. Mrs. Nichol was sitting on the porch and covered her eyes. She didn't want to see me crash her bicycle.

Not hearing a crash, she opened her eyes, and was surprised when she saw me wheeling her bicycle up the walk to her porch. I had hit the brakes just in time to stop just a few inches from the tree. How relieved I was! I knew I had to buy my own bike. I found a good used one for $10.00. I enjoyed riding my bicycle everywhere. There was never a need to lock a bicycle to a stationary object when we attended class, or prayer meeting, or went shopping. The women students stored their bicycles in the dorm basement bicycle room.

One Saturday Joyce and I rode our bicycles ten miles to Lyons, Kansas just to shop. I purchased an umbrella. Only three of the women students owned a car; few men had cars.

FALL – 1946

I was finally allowed to attend college for the entire school year. My first taste of sewing classes had encouraged me to focus on Home Economics as a major. Without a school counselor to guide me in a plan to meet all requirements for a major and a minor, I choose what I thought would be the needed classes. Among the classes I took included canning, foods, tailoring, and other domestic arts classes. My summer school class work did not include some of the basic science classes. Although I was an upper classman; I still had to take the basic science classes.

Few men had been among the college students until after the peace agreements were signed ending WWII. Then both men and women began to flood campuses including Sterling College. The free GI college program was fast changing the campus populations.

I never dated, as Mama prohibited me from that activity during my high school days. A freshman lad, Dale Stout, sat two rows behind me in biology. His brown eyes reminded me of my brother, Alvin's, deep brown eyes. Dale was from Rushville, Indiana. He said he planned to become a minister. His parents were not promoters of higher education, and had permitted him to come to college with well-worn clothes left from his high school days. He never revealed who had provided his college tuition. He confessed that he had to work many more hours than he had expected to pay for his housing, laundry, food, and other expenses.

Open house was held in the fall. It gave the guys an opportunity to roam the hallways and enter the rooms in the women's dormitory. All doors remained open during the open house hours. What an opportunity for the guys to explore as **dust sleuths** to search for any speck of dust they could fine and embarrass the ladies with their findings! With clean white handkerchiefs, they would brush the top of the door frame, the top most inaccessible part of the ceiling light globe, the floor or any other place they speculated might have a speck of dust. Even a tiny speck of dust on those white handkerchiefs was reason to harass the room residents as **dirty** housekeepers. Dale Stout with his friend, Jerry worked as one team of critics.

Dale and I began dating. We would frequently take a stroll in the evening, and soon learned we were being chaperoned. Who is following us? Who is the intruder tonight? Was our joke. We learned that without fail it was either Eleanor or Floyd (nick named "Tennessee") who would walk almost close enough to hear our conversations but not quite. We never learned why either of them was so interested in us.

In the tailoring class, I chose a brown, man-made, fake-fur fabric for a coat, a big project. Miss Oline requested the students to hand baste all seams before they were stitched on the sewing machine. I disliked hand basting. It seemed such a waste of time, as I was in a rush to complete my sewing without having to rip out the basting. I used pins to "baste" the coat pieces together except the curved neck seam. I used white basting thread. After my coat was completed, I received an A+ grade. We were always encouraged to have our tailored garments steam pressed. I sent my coat to the cleaners for the pressing even though it really did not need it.

I had worn it once then I noticed a white speck at the neckline. "What is that white speck at the neckline?" I thought as I checked my coat before I returned it to the hanger. I pulled at the white speck, out came the white basting thread, and the back neckline seam popped open. "Oh! No, I never machine stitched that seam, and I got an A+." I chuckled. It was quite a task to turn the coat inside out and stitch the neck seam in the finished coat. I chuckled to myself that my A+ coat was not completely finished until after it had been worn. I enjoyed wearing my coat but the quilted lining made it too warm to enjoy except on the coldest days.

Dr. Clark was my botany/biology professor. We were required to prepare a paper on conservation. I had mentioned the usual things: gas, wood, land, food, animals, etc. When he returned my paper, he had penned a comment: What about human conservation? Working on the farm as I had, taking care of ones self was never a consideration. It certainly made a different thought – how often do we think of conserving ourselves? Humans are not indestructible.

During the four-day Thanksgiving weekend, neither Dale nor I went home. Miss Brunton, my speech professor, had invited me and several other students to share her Thanksgiving dinner, and asked me to extend the invitation to Dale.

Just before Christmas vacation, Dale's quick temper flared up. We broke up. All the students vacated the campus to spend the Christmas holidays with their families and friends.

WINTER – SPRING – 1947

In January, the students returned to campus in full force. The student population had exploded with more servicemen and women on campus.

We had the typical central Kansas winter with blizzards, strong, icy cold winds, and bone-chilling temperatures. The unheated third-floor sleeping porch became too cold. Now we were permitted to sleep in our rooms.

I felt I had been such a horrible person for breaking off with Dale that I was miserable. Praying did not soothe my feelings of guilt. I felt I had caused someone deep sorrow. I finally gave in to my feelings and called him. We were back together again. I had been shunned and criticized call of my life at home and school. I felt comfortable to have a friend who appeared to care for me after all as Mama kept saying, "You are a terrible person" yet I had no idea what my "sins" were.

The annual dorm raid occurred early in the semester. This was a night when a girl would be "bribed" by a boy to leave an entry door unlocked. During the wee hours, when the gals were all asleep, except the traitor, the guys would storm into the hallways and up onto the sleeping porch to make sure everyone was awake. They left a nasty, stinky mess of cigarette butts that they had collected. This nasty mess was scattered on the wooden second floor hallway and first floor hallways including on the carpeted lounge area. What a mess to clean up and get the horrible stench out of the dorm! Most of the guys were thrilled with this horrendous behavior. I asked Dale if he was one of the culprits. His reply, "That was disgusting, I would never do anything like that."

Mama surprised me in a letter in February saying that she had given me a young heifer. I wrote back and told her that I was not planning to the farm after graduation. I asked her to sell my heifer and send me the money. To help pay for the feed and care until the young cow could be sold, I sent a check. I had no interest in farming, being at her beck and call, or to sharing her bed anymore. I never knew when she might hit me on the back if I got up in the middle of the night for a nature call. My only goal was to graduate from college. I never received money for my heifer. After Mama passed away, I found my uncashed check tucked under the drinking glasses in the china cabinet.

A short time later I wrote Mama and said that Dale and I were engaged. Her return letter said, "I knew you had done something terrible." My choice of a life partner would never have been acceptable to Mama, regardless of whom it may have been.

Easter break was approaching. Mama surprised me when she asked me to invite Dale to come for the four-day break. I was pleased and did not think about it being a trap set by Mama to really condemn me. Dale accompanied me for spring break.

Saturday evening, he and I drove the 25 miles to Benkelman to a program. We did not arrive home until around 11 pm. When questioned about what we were doing, I said, "I wanted him to see the spring east of Benkelman." A natural spring in this part of Nebraska was unusual. I was condemned; we were out too late.

A spring blizzard raged on Sunday, the day of our return trip to college. We had to catch the bus at Bird City to arrive at college for the beginning of classes the next day. My dad was afraid to drive on the slippery roads so he let Dale drive. The roads between Benkelman and Bird City were treacherous. My dad was afraid to drive home so he spent the night in Bird City and returned home the next day.

Mama's next letter told the whole story. She criticized me every which way she could think of. I was told we were terrible; someone (but she did not name the person) even saw us hold hands in public.

Later in the summer Mama told me, "Floy, of the Rollwitz Sunday School, wanted to give me a bridal shower." Mama said she clearly told her, "Elsieferne won't be getting married for a long, long time." Those words made me angry. I thought, "How do you know when I may get married?"

Dale and I attended the graduation ceremonies before we departed for our respective homes. I was surprised to be the recipient of a $15.00 award for "overcoming my disabilities." The campus professors chose the student who was honored with this award. I was becoming more comfortable with people, but I never really understood why I was chosen for the award.

Before Dale and I parted for our respective homes, he gave me a gold locket. His words and his actions conveyed to me that I was very important to him and that he loved me. I knew I loved him. This was the first time in my life I ever felt loved or wanted.

SUMMER – FALL – WINTER – MARRIAGE 1947

I needed two more semesters of class work to graduate in May 1948. My busy schedule always included part-time work. During my years at Sterling my work included: washing dishes in the college cafeteria, baby-sitting, typing genealogy records, ironing white shirts at 35 cents an hour, and being a summer janitor in Cooper Hall. That was the summer when a classroom needed windows opened for a 5:00 a.m Abnormal Psychology class. Also, I cleaned the second floor dorm rooms after many youth conferences each summer.

Summer school ended at the end of July. I had planned a trip to Indiana to visit Dale Stout's family. Mama had initiated the idea when she asked me to bring Dale home during Easter break. It seemed like a good idea. Since he had met my family, I should meet his family. The idea almost fell through when I commented in a letter that his mother should have extended the invitation not him. He responded with anger. A red flag I should not have ignored.

I planned to work the first semester of the coming school year, as now I only needed one more semester of credits. I found a mission school in Sky, Kentucky (later named Mountain Valley, now a name in memory). The school was in the foothills of southeastern Kentucky. Having grown up on the flat plains, I really had no concept of foothills, or that foothills were really mountains. They were willing to accept me for just the first semester, and teaching there seemed like a good experience.

I boarded the Atchison, Topeka, and Santa Fe train in Sterling. It sped east through eastern Kansas, a tunnel in Missouri, and across Illinois enroute to the Grand Central Station in Chicago, Illinois. When I arranged my trip, the schedule left 35 minutes between my arrival in Chicago and boarding the Baltimore and Ohio (B & O) train for Rushville, Indiana. I had assumed all trains arrived and departed from the same station. No problem, I thought.

After my arrival in Chicago, I asked about the Baltimore and Ohio for Rushville, Indiana. "You need to go to the Dearborn Street Station," the ticket agent said. Panic and fear! Here I was a young lady in Chicago, unfamiliar with a big city in the middle of the night, and blocks from my train station. "You can take a taxi," the agent suggested.

I asked a taxi driver to take me to the Dearborn Street Station and gave him the time my train departed. He said, "I am not sure if I can get you there in 30 minutes. I will try but you won't see much of Chicago as I'll have to go through the back streets and alleys." I was a bit uneasy as he drove very fast. We arrived just in time for me to board the train minutes, before it departed for Indianapolis enroute to Rushville.

The B & O train arrived on time in Indianapolis and to my dismay the train for Rushville had left 15 minutes earlier. When I questioned the time schedule, the agent showed me the schedule. I could not understand why the time schedule was not identical to the schedule in Sterling, Kansas. I knew I must complete my journey on the Greyhound bus.

When I phoned Dale's home, Alta, his mom, answered the phone. She said she had no idea where he was. I told her I was unable to catch the train, but would take the Greyhound bus and gave her the time of arrival. The whole family had gathered across the street from the bus station to see me when I got off the bus at the Durbin Hotel bus station in Rushville.

I met Dale's parents, Perry and Alta Stout. They were nice. They had a plain simple home that was nicer than the home I had grown up in. A large coal heating stove setting in the living room commanded the attention of all who entered the front door. The six-room house had three bedrooms, living and dining rooms, small eat-in kitchen, and a bathroom. Each room had two doors except the living room and kitchen, which had three doors each. The bathroom had only a shower and a stool, no lavatory for washing hands.

The black and yellow eat-in kitchen contained a small, coal cook stove, a built-in corner china cabinet with doors covered with fingerprints, and the only sink in the house. It was used for washing hands and shaving. The kitchen looked so bare and unfinished without curtains at the windows.

I was given the front bedroom. The simple furnishings were a double bed, dresser, and a closet with a small throw rug on the wooden floor by the bed. Every thing was plain and just bare essentials.

The Stout family gave a real feeling of family unity. Dale's Uncle Bill, Aunt Gladys, and their daughter, Dale's brother, Russell and his wife, Wilma—all welcomed me. I was very impressed. In my family there never was any display of family unity

Perry was a man who felt it was smart to make sarcastic remarks about people. He had plenty to say about the residents of Kentucky. Also, I heard many heartless remarks about the new grocery store that had been recently built across the alley from their home. It sounded like an obscene operation had moved in. I ignored them, as I did not consider his comments a criticism. That was a red flag I should not have ignored. Perry found pleasure in constantly making unkind remarks about the family. His favorite subjects were his grand children. I suspect Dale's idea of entering the ministry was an excellent subject for his criticism, although no comments were made in my presence.

Rushville was a small town of around 7,000 residents in the heart of fields of corn and soybeans. Indiana had many tall trees, green lawns, attractive shrubs, and vines grew everywhere. This was completely opposite to Nebraska's small trees, sagebrush, and soap weed (yucca) infested pastures, and smaller simple houses with no green lawns. I fell in love with the environment immediately.

Dale planned a day at the Riverside Amusement Park in Indianapolis. After we arrived, he said, "Let's ride the roller coaster." I had no idea what a roller coaster was as they were not included in the county fair rides. He chose the front seat so he could show me how brave and fearless he could be. With his arms arched high over his head, he was thrilled as the wee train zipped up and down the steep "hills." I was so terrified that I grasped tightly to the iron holding-bar anchored across our laps. He looked at me and realized this was not my kind of fun. I do not recall any other less frightening ride.

After visiting in Rushville for a few days, I had planned to take the Greyhound bus from Rushville to near Sky, Kentucky. Dale insisted I had to meet his sister, Marjorie, her husband, Arthur and their baby daughter, Wanda in Muldraugh, Kentucky. He was very proud of his little niece. Then he would take me to Sky, Kentucky.

We left Rushville for Kentucky, when we were about four miles out of Rushville a front tire blew out. Dale had an older car, and he never kept a spare. A passing motorist took us back to Rushville. Dale borrowed money from his dad to buy another tire. His dad took us back to Dale's car and helped replace the blown-out tire.

After spending the night with Dale's sister and her family, we headed for southeastern Kentucky. Cruising on the highway through central Kentucky, the road made a 90-degree curve just as we entered a bridge that crossed a river on a downhill slooping curve, my door flew open. Dale grabbed me; otherwise I might have ended up rolling across the bridge, possibly into the river below. That was terrifying.

We made the trip without further mishap through central Kentucky, then onto Highway 378 to the sign that marked the narrow winding trail that ascended up and up the foothills. It looked like a mountain to me, to the school on top was Sky, Kentucky. There were so many holes and ditches in the mountain trail road that I was afraid that Dale would break an axle or damage his car. I felt responsible because he was here for me, although I had not asked him to bring me. Now I realized why the literature stated that an ox cart was used to get the mail from the mailbox on the highway.

The school was located on top of this rugged mountain. Due to the late hour of our arrival, the tour of the buildings was postponed until the next day. We saw the spacious dining room and the administrative office that night. I was given a room on the first floor. Dale's room was in the basement of the same building. When the receptionist told me about the bats in the dormitory, I knew immediately I could not stay. I have a horrific fear of bats. I also realized that if I stayed, the winter snows could block the roads and prevent my return to college in January. I was so disappointed that tears pooled in my eyes. This position had seemed very important but we left the next morning.

During the drive back to Rushville, many thoughts collided in my thinking. "What was I going to do now?" I was vexed. I recalled a remark that my dad had made about Faye, one of my grade school teachers. She had reminisced at school about day trip that she and her fiancé had taken to the eastern part of Nebraska. When I mentioned the trip at the supper table, my dad's remark was, "He'd better marry her." I was puzzled but that remark still bothered me. Now I had made a long trip with a man. Did that mean we had to get married just because we had shared a trip together? I was confused.

No serious conversation was shared during the return trip. I could hear Mama telling me again, "You are a terrible person" or "You sinned against God because you did not keep your promise to the school." I felt trapped. I had no desire to return home to Mama. However, I never shared my thoughts. Silence prevailed as neither of us instigated any conversation.

It was dusk when we arrived in Rushville. Dale's parents had gone to visit their daughter, Marjorie, in Kentucky. I stated that I wanted to get a room at the Durbin Hotel. "You don't need to do that," he said. "You have your room and I have mine." I was so tired that I gave in, but I knew he'd better stay in his room. We brought our suitcases into the house and prepared for bed. Before he went to bed, he knocked at my door, and asked to come in. "No!" I firmly said. He waited and waited then finally left for his room at the other end of the house.

Dale did not want me to leave Rushville. Finally he said, "Let's get married now and not wait. I don't want you to teach. You won't mind if you don't graduate with your class." I was caught off guard. I had not considered marriage until I had finished college; I really did not want to teach either. When we met, he kept talking about becoming a minister. He had said, "A young man in a wheel chair, who he had met at Synod School at Hanover, Indiana earlier in 1947 had inspired him." Dale enrolled at Sterling College as the first step of this goal, possibly at the suggestion of his pastor, the Reverend O. Rupe, a Sterling Alumni. Now Dale said, "I'm not going back to Sterling." He grumbled that he felt he'd had been unjustly treated with his grades. He was going back to work with his dad in carpentry work. I thought he was a committed Christian as I believed only someone with strong faith and devotion to God would consider devoting a lifetime serving as a minister. I really believed he'd continue his plans as he'd been given a small church to preach in every Sunday. If not the ministry, at least continue some additional education. I felt it would be an honor to serve as a minister's wife, a partner in the ministry.

I had no alternative plans for September 1947 to January 1948. I was emotionally confused, physical exhausted, and in a whirl without a plan to reach my goal to graduate. I **did not** have the time to rationalize the whole situation. I considered his proposal while I protested each of his arguments for immediate marriage, but he always came back with many arguments for marriage. My strongest argument was: "If we get married now, everyone will think, I have to get married. I don't have to get married." He, like Mama, always had an answer that made my feelings and protests unimportant— almost ashamed that I did not agree. Finally, I very foolishly agreed.

Dale had frequently said, "I wished we were married" during the spring semester that I felt like a monster with my lack of interest. Many of the students were making wedding plans. It seemed wrong not to be doing the same. I reasoned it would be a way to get away from Mama, which I knew would not make her happy. She had even been demeaning my dad's family name "Mendenhall" as if they were a family of criminals. I was ashamed to bear the name and wanted to get rid of it and hide. One time she wrote that my dad had "Downs Syndrome" because of his temper. I challenged her. She said someone had told her that because of his quick temper so she passed the "gossip" on as fact. I wrote that she should get the facts correct and not be judging other people. I quoted from the King James Version of the Bible: "Judge not, that ye be not judged. For with what judgment ye judge, ye shall be judged . . . ." Matthew 7:1, 2. She passed off the scripture quotation with a comment that it did not apply to her, because she was a "chosen prophet of God."

Dale wanted to go to the Justice of Peace and be married immediately, but I said, "I want a church wedding." That displeased him, but he reluctantly agreed. Then I said, "First, I am going home to tell Mama my plans." I left immediately for Nebraska.

When I arrived in Benkelman, I wondered how I was going to get out to the farm 25 miles away as no one knew I was coming home. With my empty cardboard suitcase I started walking north on Highway 61. It was not long before a vehicle stopped. The driver identified himself and he was a gentleman who I had heard my dad talk about. He asked if he could take me to my destination. I agreed to let him take me home. Mama was aghast to see me come home riding with a man who she did not know. I thanked him and went into the house. He visited with my dad a few minutes before leaving.

I told Mama of my plans. She surprised me with, "That's alright. The Frenchman Valley School on Highway 61 needs a teacher. You can teach at that school." As usual Mama had her "school-needs-a-teacher-antenna" tuned in.

"No, Mom," I replied. "I am going to live with my husband." That was the first time I had said "No" to Mama since I had made a promise to myself when I was eight years old.

That incident occurred because we were going to a pitch-in meal. Mama had baked cup cakes. They were burned when she removed them from the oven. "Just cut off the burnt bottom and ice the top. They will be good enough," she instructed.

Smarty me, I retorted, "They are not fit to eat." They were burned so much that even the tops tasted burned. Mama went into the front room and cried. When I saw how my words had affected her, I vowed never to challenge her instructions again. What a mistake!

While I was enroute home on the bus, I had thought of the wedding dress that I would make during the week I was home. Actually I was excited with anticipation as I thought of my wedding dress. My plan to make a wedding dress became a "pipe dream." The whole week I was home I had to help my mama and my dad install plasterboard in her little house in Benkelman. This was the house that she had built for my brothers to live in while they attended high school. The one-room house had been rented. It needed repairs in preparation for a new occupant. I was quite astounded to see bed bugs everywhere, and so thankful none crawled onto my clothing.

I was taken to Ogallala, Nebraska, to catch the Greyhound bus. I wanted to shop for a blouse to wear with the new mint green suit I'd made during the summer. Mama looked around, but I did not realize that she was looking for a wedding dress for me. When I told her about my suit, she replied, "Married in green, ashamed to be seen." I walked past a two-piece ivory lace dress on sale for $13.00, and commented that it was nice. She had bought it before I could say "No." She felt good but I was disappointed. She had had her choice as usual.

We were married on September 10, 1947 in the United Presbyterian Church in Rushville, Indiana with the Reverend Orus Rupe officiating at the small wedding. When I stepped out of my bedroom dressed in my out-of-season, lace dress to go to the church, I was disappointed to see Dale's parents sitting as usual in their rocking chairs. I related my surprise and disappointment. Alta, Dale's mother, indicated that they had not been invited. I stated that I had not sent invitations to Dale's family but had asked him to verbally extend the invitation. I sent a note to my brother, Alvin, as I knew I would not be allowed to drive to his farm to tell him. Dale's parents came in the clothes they had on when I left the house. I never understood them.

After the ceremony, we went to our tiny house. A few minutes later a loud knock sounded on the door. When Dale opened the door, his family members and friends greeted him ready for chivery fun. It was the custom of the time to celebrate a wedding with a parade down Main Street with the couple in an old trailer with horns honking. The crowd was disappointed when they discovered that I had changed out of my lace dress which could have been ruined in the trailer. The group had planned no refreshments. We were returned to our tiny house after the parade.

The next morning Dale refused to get up and go to work. I could not understand as no one at my parent's home was allowed to stay in bed after being called. I called and called him. Finally, I went back to bed and let his breakfast get cold. When he finally got up, he angrily questioned, "Why didn't you get me up?" Perry, his dad, and his brother had stopped and were patiently waiting for Dale to go to work. He changed and was no longer interested in companionship or friendly conversation but never lacked in critical remarks.

I puzzled all day – should I pack up and leave while he was at work? I had taken my marriage vows seriously and felt a divorce was the greatest of all sins. I did not go, but I was so confused.

During the next few weeks things were rocky with the biggest problem being Dale's lack of interest in getting up to go to work. He kept saying, "You didn't get me up." He never accepted that responsibility for himself.

He complained all the time that I did not eat enough to suit him. He had an unreal obsession with food. He could eat two big plates full of food, then before bedtime eat a huge bowl of popcorn and nearly pint of ice cream topped with peanuts or peanut butter and gobs of chocolate syrup. He never gained weight. Such huge quantities of food would have made me sick.

Dale was no longer interested in attending church, while at Sterling college he was always there. I tried to establish a time of family Bible reading and prayer, but he made sure that did not happen. Mornings were an impossible time; evenings I was so exhausted that I would go to sleep reading. Also, I discovered that Dale was a night person while I was a morning person, not a good combination.

Six weeks after we were married, he broke a promise that he had solemnly made before we were married. He said, "I just can't live without smoking." That was another heartbreak. He knew cigarette smoke made me sick but only his feelings were of any concern. I seriously considered leaving during his absence. But I remembered Mama's words "**Don't rock the boat**; accept what the other fellow demands." I did not leave. I have always felt his dad's cutting remarks influenced his actions on smoking and college. Many years later I demanded no smoking in the house; I soon found that family unity prevailed as Dale's family all told me how mean I was not to allow him to smoke in his own home. I ignored them.

Shortly after that smoking deal, I said, "You are doing what your want – smoking; now I'm going back to Sterling to get my degree." He did not want me to go but he had to accept my decision however reluctantly, or give up smoking permanently.

During the cold, winter days his dad did not schedule enough carpentry work to keep himself and his two sons, Dale and Russell, busy and with income. Dale realized that he had to have money coming in. He obtained a job delivering bakery products for the Meckes Bakery, a local business. He was delighted with this job as it was night work. He wanted me to go on the truck with him all the time but I could not be up all night and sleep days.

His family always celebrated Christmas with a cedar tree they'd cut in the woods and gaily decorated, gifts, a big meal, and a family get-together. No giving of thanks, or attendance at a religious service. The women always had a day of work: preparing the food, serving it, and cleaning up afterwards.

At my home all the outward signs of Christmas were absent but I was always required to give thanks everyday before we ate even though there were no religious services available to attend.

Dale insisted that we had to follow his family's tradition and have a tree too. He found a small cedar tree in the woods to decorate. There were other traditions that we had to follow. That included purchasing groceries from the same store his folks did because they could get groceries on credit—the cockroaches in that store made me cringe; buying hardware from Hayden's Hardware, the most expensive store in Rushville; and buying winter heating fuel on time. Interest was not charged by any of those businesses. I was told many times that they did not accept charity. Yet they did not see charging groceries, hardware items, and heating fuel without paying interest was charity. In my understanding, it was charity.

STERLING COLLEGE – 1948

In January, Dale took me and my two cardboard suitcases to the Greyhound bus station in Rushville, Indiana. We learned the bus had just left, but according to our watches there was plenty of time. Dale drove part way to Indianapolis catch the bus at one of its many stops. At last I was on my way back to achieve my goal of a college degree.

When I registered at Sterling College, my deposit of $5.00, which reserved my room, had been misfiled. Finally it was found; otherwise I would not have had a room. My teaching money paid for my expenses. One semester's tuition costs were $100.00 and included lab fees; room rent was $45.00 a semester. Food was purchased from the school cafeteria at a very modest fee. I purchased meal tickets for $5.00, and tried to eat on $5.00 a week, but just could not make it. I do not recall the cost of books but that may have been part of the tuition costs.

I felt confident my Home Economics classes met the requirements for a Home Economics Major. Without guidance from a counselor, I had consulted the college catalogue. But when I signed up for experimental cooking, I was told my credits would not qualify me for this class which was a required course for a Home Economics Major. Finally, I was allowed to take the class, even though I had not taken chemistry. I had not taken college chemistry because my high school did not offer chemistry. The only high school science class was general science. I had numerous other science classes in college. It was agreed that my major would be Home Economics/Biology with minors in English and Bible. I do not recall the other classes I enrolled in for this final semester.

The women's dormitory was overflowing; but one room was available in The Annex, a house that was across the street from the campus. A professor and his wife were the house parents. Marge and Sara were occupants of the downstairs bedroom, while Helen and Doris occupied the upstairs room next to mine; I had no roommate. The rooms were nice and large. The Annex girls were a jolly group.

Soon special student, Virginia B. of Cairo, Egypt arrived. She was assigned to be my roommate. We gave her a royal welcome and admired her beautiful sheets and pillowcases adorned with intricate hand-embroidery designs.

Virginia was accustomed to a completely different life style than all the other residents of the Annex. Her family had servants to do the labor, while the women occupied their time with hand embroidery and other luxuries.

She was not cooperative. When she and I were both at the study table, she would insist that my desk lamp shade be turned so the light shown right up into my eyes. I never could convince her that the light should shine straight down on the desk. Late night studying was not on my schedule. I went to bed around 9:00 p.m. but Virginia kept things buzzing into the wee hours. She'd even go into our walk-in closet and throw things around in the middle of the night. This noise bothered Doris and Helen in the next room.

The next thing I knew I was called into the office of Mrs. Tidrick, the Dean of Women. She asked why I was being so "ugly" to Virginia. I relayed my side of the story. She said, "I wondered what the problem could be as you have never had a problem here." With all the dorm rooms filled, there was no place for either of us to move. At first Mrs. Tidrick suggested that perhaps Joyce would not mind sharing her single room with me. I could not do that as I felt like I would be imposing on Joyce, my best friend. Another suggestion was that I could take one of the partially finished rooms in the basement of the Annex. The unfinished room had box springs and mattress, walk-in closet, a study table and chair, and book shelves. I had everything I needed including my desk lamp. I have always wondered why I was the one who had to move to a different room.

There were giant cockroaches in the laundry room next door. As soon as I moved in, I purchased some roach powder and made a barrier line around the perimeter of my room including across the doorway. The roaches never crossed the barrier.

Dale kept writing saying he was so lonesome and begged me to return. He said, "The neighbors were watching him like a hawk." I think he imagined that but I was feeling badly about "poor Dale" and had considered giving up my quest. I talked with Mrs. Tidrick, about getting a refund. She immediately expressed her opinion that "poor Dale" could take care of himself, and I should stay in school, which I did.

In my experimental cooking class, we were to experiment for the best method to make light, fluffy, melt-in-your-mouth biscuits. After class I brought the biscuits home and broke them into halves, sprinkled a generous serving of roach powder on and around each half as I placed the biscuits on the floor in the laundry room. The next day the roach population had been greatly reduced.

Joyce and the dorm girls honored me with a generous bridal shower one evening. I set my beautiful gifts on the bookshelves. I had stored some snacks in a glass sauce pan with a matching lid. When I lifted the lid from the pan, it split in two. I have no idea why, as I had never had the opportunity to cook with it.

With the returning service men and women, the college had relaxed the—no dancing—regulations during the fall semester. The gym rocked with fun and laughter during the folk dancing events. I loved folk dancing and participated at every event possible.

Another of my experimental cooking projects was "How to keep the bottom crust of a cherry pie crisp." I made several single serving pies each crust was treated differently: one was brushed with melted butter; another was coated with egg white, one without any coating, and one baked before the filling was added. Each crust had same cherry pie filling. I do not recall which method resulted with the crispiest crust. This experiment concluded near the end of March. I was telling my house mates about all of my cherry pies. Then Marge and Sara said, "We are having a party this evening, will you come?" I thought this would be an excellent opportunity to share my cherry pies. I disliked tossing good food into the garbage, better to share it. "May I bring my pies?" I asked. They agreed wholeheartedly.

While I do not recall all of the activities for the party, I vividly recall the refreshments. Our hostesses served chocolate Oreo cookies. They looked delicious but one bite and my taste buds rebelled. I kept wondering "Why do these cookies taste so peculiar?" All of the guests politely ate the cookies without a negative comment. I quickly served my cherry pies. We graciously thanked our hostesses for a wonderful party. After we returned to our respective rooms, I cautiously asked, "Helen, did you notice that peculiar taste in those cookies?"

"Did I ever!" Doris quickly returned, "I thought you were never going to serve those cherry pies."

Helen glanced at their calendar and proclaimed, "Today is April 1." We had attended an April Fool's Day party without realizing it. Were the guests fooled? Or were the hostesses? Then we realized that the peculiar taste in the cookies was white ivory soap.

Graduation was May 31, 1948. The weekend before graduation I went home with Dorothy and Ellen to Hutchinson, Kansas to enjoy my last weekend with them. What a surprise to have Dale appear at their door just as we were setting down for the Sunday noon meal! Unknown to me, he left early and had driven straight through from Rushville, Indiana to Sterling, Kansas over 700 miles. He was surprised and unhappy to find me off campus.

I don't recall how he said he had learned that I had gone to Hutchinson. We did not need to sign out in the Annex, as was required at Campbell Hall. He was invited to join us. After dinner, he and I returned to Sterling. Since I had a separate basement room, he did not need to find a sleeping room. He went to bed immediately and slept continuously for 22 hours.

My next surprise was a letter from Mama stating that she was coming to my graduation! The Greyhound bus route went by the campus. Aunt Alma and Uncle Melvin from Norton, Kansas, also were among the attendees. I was so happy that part of my family was present. I believe I was the first person in my family to attend or graduate from college.

When I introduced Mama to Mrs. Tidrick, the house mother, Mrs. Tidrick said, "You have a wonderful daughter, you should be proud of her." I do not recall Mama's reply other than a nod of her head. I hoped she was proud of me.

I said a silent prayer as I received my diploma that afternoon, "Thank you, God, for giving me strength to persevere." I had at last achieved my goal!

Aunt Alma and Uncle Melvin had a larger car than Dale's Model A Ford coup. They invited Mama to ride with them to their home at Norton, Kansas, where we would pick her up to take her home.

During the next week in Nebraska, Dale and I visited my brother, Alvin and his family at his farm near Haigler, Nebraska. Dale helped with corn planting. This was the first time I visited my brother's home. When I drove the family car, Mama controlled where I went.

Then we visited Uncle Andy and Aunt Grace. Uncle Andy was a character! Dale had been warned about Uncle Andy's tricks. We were invited to share a meal; we accepted. But when Uncle Andy tried to shove Dale's thumb in the mashed potatoes, it didn't happen. Then Uncle Andy passed Dale the gravy bowl and, he tried again to shove the bowl to get gravy all over Dale's thumb, and again he was unsuccessful. Then Uncle Andy said, "Somebody has been talking!" as he looked at me. Everyone laughed. Uncle Andy's habit of always shoving a guest's thumb into food was his trademark. He enjoyed embarrassing his guests.

I had told Dale to be sure he always had a tank of gas before we left Benkelman to go to my parent's farm, "There is plenty," he said, "around a half tank." I tried to convince him that it was a long distance between gas pumps in the sand hills, but he would not listen. I believe Uncle Andy even asked if he had enough gas.

We left Uncle Andy's home and headed northeast towards Enders, Nebraska, a small town near a new large man-made lake. We had gone probably 10 miles when the car coughed and died. Sure enough—out of gas—and we were out in the farming area. A windmill stood nearby at the edge of a large field where a cloud of dust indicated that a farmer was in the field. Dale walked over to the windmill, disconnected the shaft from the wheel, and then tried to hand pump some water, but he couldn't. After 15-20 minutes, the farmer shut off his tractor and came over to see if he could help us. Dale mentioned he'd tried to get a drink of water but couldn't. "I am not surprised," the farmer replied, "That well is 256 feet deep." He was able to spare us enough gas to get to Enders where Dale filled the tank. He learned – it is a long distance between gas pumps in the Nebraska sand hills.

Mama appeared to accept my marriage. Dale and I headed east to our home in Indiana. All appeared well while we were there. I left feeling good but the truth was learned when Mama refused to write to me for four years.

EPILOGUE

After we returned to our home in Rushville, Indiana, Dale joined his dad in carpentry work. His mother evidently had a strong influence over Dale for him to endure the work that he hated. He complained that the work caused his neck, shoulders, and back to hurt. Little modern equipment was provided to lessen the tough, heavy jobs. He hated to wear warm garments for protection in the cold, winter weather. It was so much easier to complain that his neck was hurting because the weather had been cold and windy instead of putting the hood of his sweatshirt up over his cap to protect his neck from the weather. I told him I did not want to hear his complaints as he had a hood to protect his neck. Dale seemed unable to do tasks on his own without having to run to ask his dad.

Dale's dad seemed to have less and less work during the cold months. Dale tried his own hand at carpentry repair work but that was not profitable. He tried several other jobs, but finally stayed with trucking. First, it was with the Meckes Bakery; then he drove for a friend, next he purchased his own truck, and began long distance hauling. Finally, he sold his truck because it was not profitable, and drove for the Fraley Trucking Company, Rushville, Indiana.

Our marriage was very rocky. On weekends he wanted to sleep until afternoon; on work days, he'd stay up until midnight, then fight instead of getting up for work the next morning. Anger remained with him much of the time. When I tried to talk to him, he'd slam the door hard as he left the house, jumped into his vehicle, and spun the wheels as he sped away. I'd sit down in tears blaming myself. As Mama had always said, "I was a terrible person," so I felt I was to blame for his anger. I could do nothing to please him.

When I'd call him to get up for breakfast, he swung his arms towards me often hitting me. When he did get up, I was blamed for not getting him up. I told him he had to get himself up, but he never acknowledged being called. Sleep for Dale was difficult. He snored loudly; his arms and legs were in constant motion. He'd snort and quit breathing then make loud gasping sounds and jerky body movements when his breath returned. This would happen many times each night. Sometimes in his jerky body movement sessions, he'd fall out of bed. Now I hear this condition referred to as "sleep apnea." In his mind though, there was nothing wrong with him. One day just after he got up he began to hit me. I told him in no uncertain words there would be no more of that or "he would be sorry." Yet I had no idea what I would do. I was thankful that he did not repeat his actions.

Finally, after years of going with little sleep, which affected my health, I finally purchased twin beds. The old wired-together bed frame and mattress were traded in. (The rails were wired together because they'd bow out and let the wooden slats fall on the floor. Many times he had to put the bed together during the night. Finally, one night I said, "This is it. I'm sleeping on the couch." The next day he used number nine wire to pull the rails tight to the wooden slats.) He **blew up** when he came home from a trucking trip and found twin beds in the bedroom. I believe the effect would have been quieter, if I'd handed him divorce papers. "I have the right to sleep too," I told him. He felt I had no right to spend **his** money, or do anything without **his** permission.

After his explosion about the twin beds, I said, "You tried to kill both Helen and me three days before she was born." He opened his mouth to repeat his usual excuse that "he did not know what he was doing;" then closed it as I continued, "You knew exactly what you were doing." I never called him again to get up. He learned to use an alarm clock which sometimes would ring for an hour before he got up and shut it off.

It was also about this time that he learned that I would no longer get up in the middle of the night to change the wet bed because he couldn't get up to go to the bathroom. It was surprising how quickly that stopped when I said, "This is it! Sleep in your wet bed. I'm sleeping on the couch." A miracle! No more wet bed. No more excuses that "he couldn't help it" were heard.

I do not recall what reminded Dale of this incident but he was laughing when he hold about this incident involving Russell, his brother, when they slept in the same bed in their parents home. He said

> "Russell had returned home after completing a tour of duty during WWII. He and I again shared the bed in the front bedroom. He usually slept next to the wall, but this night he had come in late. I had already taken his usual place. The next morning when Mom came into the bedroom to get me up, she grabbed the nearest ear, gave it a hard, quick twist."
>
> Chuckling he continued, "Russell came up out of the bed with no kind words for Mom."

I wondered, "Does he swing his arms toward sounds to defend himself from morning ear twisting? Was this a common every day practice?" No wonder he always strikes out at a voice.

It was several years after we were married when visiting with one of Dale's aunts that I learned Dale's dad would knock his mom down. Also, they would lock Dale, a pre-schooler, out of the house when his dad wasn't working, and the older children were at school. Dale would have to go over to this aunt's house for a drink of water. Another relative verified the abusive behavior in the home.

Our first daughter, Helen, arrived in July after a difficult delivery. (Dale had hit me hard on the abdomen three days earlier when I tried to call him for work around 11:00 p.m. I was stunned. The phone rang for an hour. I couldn't and didn't answer it. I was sick.) I was so tense from nerves that the baby had to be delivered with the aid of forceps. The forceps slipped and left a long scar across the Helen's cheek. Dr. Worth, attending physician, apologized for the scar and encouraged me to stay in the hospital for three days after the delivery. I agreed as I was exhausted. Dale, a penny pincher, was very distressed when Dr. Worth stated that I had agreed to stay. After I went home, he brought a young girl home to help me. She was lazy and did not even want to diaper the baby. She was promised and received the same wages as an experienced helper.

Dale always wanted a child but soon after he became a father, he said, "Babies are too messy. I am not goin' to help with her, that's her mother's job." So Helen was my baby to care for. I felt he should at least help on weekends when he was home. One Sunday morning I asked him to give Helen her morning cereal. She quit eating before she had eaten all that was prepared; he thought she should eat it all. So he boxed her jaws to get her to finish all of the cereal.

We were at his parent's home later that day for a family dinner. He bragged how he had made Helen eat her cereal. Dale's obsession for food was so unreal. His sister-in-law, Wilma was aghast when she heard his bragging. She did not mince words to tell him how abusive that was. I provided for all of Helen's care from then on.

I was thankful that Helen appeared to have no after affects of that severe blow to my abdomen before her birth and she was healthy. I had been very sick during my pregnancy.

We had purchased the house the year before. After we had lived in it about two months, I noticed termites so numerous that they were making their mud tunnels on the wallpapered bedroom walls. Dale and his Uncle Bill treated the house with creosote to kill the termites because he knew it would get rid of the insects. Dale did not consider that those fumes were harmful, and always claimed he could not smell anything. When the house was closed for winter heating, the fumes were horrific. That almost wiped out his wife and baby. There was no money to provide a change of place for me to live and no way to convince him that the fumes were harmful. I will always wonder if her many allergies were a result of those fumes.

Soon after her birth, I noticed mosquitoes were feasting on Helen. To protect her from those insects, I removed the sheer, living room door curtain and draped it over the baby buggy to protect her. The mosquitoes feasted on Dale while he slept, no welts were left from their feasting, and they feasted until they were too full to fly.

Two years later, I was pregnant with our second child with delivery date near. Dale had returned to truck driving and was home from his night of driving. He was exhausted and was soon sound asleep. I did not feel well and lay on the couch in the living room to watch Helen play.

Janet, daughter of our Milroy grocer, had asked me to make her a sun dress. She was getting ready to return to college and came for her dress. When I stood up to get her the dress; blood gushed everywhere. I headed for the bathroom leaving a trail of blood. Two-year old, Helen was frightened and ran around the living room saying "Oh, Oh, Oh," between her little sobs.

Janet grabbed Helen and ran to the Powers' home across the street to call Dr. Worth, our town doctor. Mrs. Powers came immediately and said that Janet was taking care of Helen and would bring her back when she was called. Mrs. Worth, my doctor's wife and office nurse came immediately. She stated that Doctor Worth would arrive in a few minutes as he was at the hospital in Rushville, eight miles away.

When I returned to the living room from the bathroom, I was shaking so much I could hardly walk. I sat down; I could do nothing, not even think clearly. I was so frightened. It was like I was in a horrible dream. This was just one week before the baby's projected due date. I had had no labor pains. Dr. Worth arrived and immediately said; "You need to go to the hospital for a C-section." I was worried about myself and my baby with surgery involved. The hospital and the surgeon were immediately alerted. The ambulance, a funeral hearse, was called for the trip to the hospital; it was a rough ride.

All of this commotion happened in the living room with the bedroom door wide open, but Dale snoozed away. Yes, he was always very tired after a night of truck driving. The soundness of his sleep was normal. When all was readied for me to leave, Mrs. Worth went into the bedroom to awaken Dale. She shook him several times and commented that she thought he'd never wake up. Janet brought Helen back as I ready to leave; Helen now had a coloring book with a small box of crayons.

Dale was given the news that I would leave immediately for the hospital by ambulance. He took Helen and her clothes for her visit with Aunt Wilma (arrangements I'd had a made earlier for my hospital stay). I had not expected to spend a week in the hospital.

A healthy baby girl, Ruth, arrived by C-section around 5:30 p.m. Dale was unhappy as he wanted a boy. He constantly complained during the girls' years at home that he was outnumbered.

Dale and Aunt Wilma brought Helen to see me at the hospital once during the week I was there. I was in a wheel chair when I met them in the hospital lobby. Helen wanted to sit on my lap but her dad said, "Mommy has a sore tummy and you can't sit in her lap." Helen was too young to understand, as she stood by my chair silently begging for her mommy's arms and lap. After all I'd been whisked away in a strange vehicle while she was taken to Aunt Wilma's home and left. It was a shock to all. She missed her mommy's hugs. Aunt Wilma picked her up and sat her in my lap. Both she and I enjoyed her time in my lap. I gave her a big hug. I often wonder what went through her little mind during that most unusual frightening week. There was no way to prepare her for the unknown.

When Dale and Helen came to take Ruth and me to his parent's home a week later, Helen wanted us to leave the baby at the hospital.

Dale's family fought health insurance with a passion. During the previous winter, Dale had worked in a factory in Connersville, Indiana about four months. All the employees and their families were covered by health insurance. It was a blessing as this insurance covered the expenses for the week's stay for my baby and me at the hospital, and the doctor, and surgeon. Total costs were around $600.00. We had no extra money.

After the week in the hospital, Ruth and I stayed at Dale's parents' home for another week. His mom took care of us. Aunt Wilma brought Helen every day, then returned in the evening and took Helen back to her house. I was able to be up but was very weak. I had had a blood clot in my right leg, so I had to be very careful.

When Grandma bathed Ruth the first time, she screamed. I ignored it as I lay in bed, thinking she did not like to be bathed. The second day I walked into the living room as Grandma was preparing the bath water. "I'll bathe her today," I offered. I sat down and Grandma gave Ruth to me, then she took the wash pan of water from the top of the heating stove and set it on a chair next to me. I put my hand into the prepared bath water and explained, "This water is much too hot to bathe a baby. No wonder she screams when she's bathed."

"I did not want her to catch cold," Grandma replied. I could see that a baby made Grandma very nervous.

That evening when Dale came in, I requested that he get some baby oil and cotton balls. "Ruth was being burned with the hot water bath." I explained softly. There were no more hot water baths; no more screaming baths either.

At the end of the week, my two girls, and I went to our home in Milroy. The first night home I was alone with both girls—babies. I was concerned and worried as I was so weak. I cried as I clung to Dale before he left for work. The next morning Dale brought a young girl from Rushville to help, but as usual she was inexperienced. She did an acceptable job with the washing and cooking. Near the end of the week, after she had completed the washing, she said, "We are out of cold water but there is plenty of hot water." I knew our 30 foot hand-dug well would run dry when excess water was used but did not realize she had used that much.

I thought, "Oh, no!" Then I questioned, "Where does the water come from for the hot water?" She stopped and thought, then agreed the water came from the well. This hand-dug well did not stay dry for long yet only provided a limited amount of water. She stayed a week, and then I was on my own. I needed help with the laundry for another month.

Mrs. King, a neighbor lady, came a day later and offered to help. "I can sweep off the front porch," she said. No one came to the front door as everyone came to the side porch door, the door to our living room.

"Why?" I asked, "We never use it." That was the only help offered by the neighbors. I believe everyone in town knew the circumstances around the birth of my baby, but no one offered help, not even members of my church.

However, a neighbor who lived across the street came seeking a donation for funeral flowers for a person I did not know. She explained that everyone else in that part of town had donated and she didn't want to leave us out so she added our names. I had no money to give. Milroy was a small town with a population less than 1,000 residents.

I had been given a blood transfusion while in the hospital. The rule was two pints of blood were needed to replace the pint used. Dale finally donated a pint, and then he sat up too quickly on the bed. Immediately, he became dizzy, fell, hit his head, and bent his glasses. He was so angry, and said he was not going to donate any more blood. He never asked any of his co-workers, or family members to donate either.

The hospital kept billing us for the second pint of blood. After a year, I asked if I could replace that pint. I was accepted. I left the children with my neighbor, Marjorie M. and never told Dale about it. At the next family gathering, he bragged that the hospital had finally quit billing for the pint of blood. I calmly said, "They shouldn't bill us because I donated the needed pint." He shut up.

Whenever Dale was doing carpentry work, money was always very limited. He told me that he bragged to the people he worked for that he didn't need money. Both girls were in school. I finally turned to substitute teaching at the school across the street from our home just to help meet the monthly bills which included our mortgage payments. My part-time work made him so angry that he got drunk. The planned trip to Nebraska to celebrate Christmas with my brother and his family was cancelled. I blamed myself for his behavior; I ended up very sick.

I had to raise my two girls basically alone, as Dale was gone driving a truck much of the time. Sometimes he was gone six weeks at a time. As a non-union driver, he received the lower pay. We were usually scraping the bottom each month to keep the bills paid. His hotel and food bills came out of his wages, too. During the summer months, we always had the previous winter's heating fuel and groceries to pay for.

If the girls or I were sick, I always had to manage on my own. Dale's mother was afraid of any illness. One time his parents did bring me a prescription, but left it on the porch and immediately left. When Ruth and I had chicken pox, at the same time, Dale happened to be home. He cooked a meal of potatoes, sausage, and green beans in the same pan, a dish that everyone liked, but before he served it, he poured a generous amount of catsup over it. My mouth and throat were so filled with chicken pox sores that I could not eat anything, only cry with pain from the sting of the catsup. His mother had never taught him survival skills. He believed a wife would always be there to care for him, and she would never need any care.

Enough about that phase of my marriage. Dale demanded that I would not work away from home. Fact was he did not approve of me going anywhere. I was to stay home **period**. He was an impulsive person and made decisions without thought of the consequence, discussion with me, or the financial needs to meet his decisions.

Since I did not work away from home, I turned to my church the Milroy United Presbyterian Church, for friendship and out-of-home activities. I volunteered as choir director, Sunday school superintendent, Sunday school teacher, church secretary, organist, choir member, and Youth leader. Later, after the Milroy United Presbyterian Church closed due to lack of attendance; I attended the First Presbyterian Church in Rushville, Indiana. Here I was ordained an Elder, and a Deacon, and elected Clerk of the Session (the keeper of the official church records). Also, worked with the children and even wrote my own Sunday school materials.

Beside my church volunteer activities, I served as: 4-H leader; 4-H judge; American Cancer Society patient transporter; Hospital Auxiliary (making little horses for hospitalized children); community news correspondent for the *Rushville Republican* newspaper, VBS (Vacation Bible School) teacher and director, and Home Economics Club member. I also participated in Home Economics State Fair dress reviews with my creatively designed garments in the professional category. Dale resented all of these volunteer involvements.

Dale objected to the girls' involvement in 4-H, 4-H camp, or piano lessons, or baby sitting, and going to college. He'd throw temper tantrums and scream at me when I allowed them the privilege of any of these activities. He believed they should marry and be subject to a man's orders for the rest of their lives. I disagreed. I am very proud of them as they both went to college with scholarships and graduated.

One day in the late 1970's as Dale and I were motoring to Ruth's home in Bloomington, Indiana, he expounded against the Affirmative Action Law that required employers to employ blacks, women, and ethnics. This law emphasized that everyone should have a chance to work. Coming from a racist family, he felt strongly that only white males had a right to work. He turned to me and stated, "That is right, isn't it?" I ignored his question as I pondered how I could tactfully reply. He turned his face to me and repeated the question with more emphasis, "That's right, isn't it?"

I calmly replied, "I don't know since I am one of them." He shut up. That topic was never broached again. He believed a wife should be voiceless, barefooted, pregnant, and penniless.

I had wanted to leave Dale so many times before the girls were born; there was no safe place to go. I would not go back to Mama and there were no shelters as are available now in the 2000's. Loans were not available for females and there were few good job opportunities. The available jobs were very low pay, and many male bosses demanded sexual favors for employment. After the girls became part of the family, I was threatened that if I left him, he'd find me and . . . But it was acceptable, if he had a woman at the many truck stops and in between. After all he was a **white male** with the right to do as he pleased.

I needed help. I had turned to my doctor, Dr. Worth he indicated that I had caused Dale's problem. I went to my minister, but he only spoke of "the hell of a divorce." He was referring to his divorce before his call to Rushville. I tried a counselor in Rushville. She ordered me to do things with a demanding tone, "You shall . . ." which was like hearing Mama and Dale all over again. Again, no help. After much suffering and crying, I was so distraught that one day in Rushville, I could not drive home from Rushville to Milroy because of tears. My pastor, the Reverend Ron, referred me to an Indianapolis counselor. This counselor insisted that I join a support group that met in the evenings. "No," I replied, "I am afraid to drive in Indianapolis at night." This would have been a 50 mile trip one-way from my home to downtown Indianapolis. I continued to suffer much emotional stress and physical health problems. I felt trapped. There was no one to talk with.

My self-esteem had been destroyed by Mama's frequent remarks "You are a terrible person" and "You have sinned, "—I knew not what for. All of that made positive thinking next to impossible. Mama's thoughts flashed back to the days of her childhood, repeating words she'd heard during her years in her Uncle Jacob and Aunt Caroline's home. She thought that was the proper way to make me work harder **to make something of myself.** I believed that I had to be perfect. My husband was constantly criticizing me until felt I it was useless to make a decision because regardless of my decision, it would be deemed wrong.

My self-esteem had plummeted to the bottom – I wondered – Could I be successful with correspondence courses? A little voice inside me kept nagging me that I should try correspondence courses to refresh my thinking and escape a little while from the turmoil. One class was a creative writing class. The instructor must have been a young, male, graduate student. The lesson material contained examples of stories using many four-lettered, street language words. I wrote to the instructor and stated that a teacher should not instruct students to use "four-lettered, street language words" in writings.

Instead they should set good examples, using correct English not trashy words." I took several other interesting classes. It was with this approach that I slowly began to rebuild my confidence.

I had an opportunity to write the Milroy community news for the *Rushville Republican* newspaper. I needed to phone people each week to collect news and in this way I became acquainted with members of the community. That was my greatest moral boaster. I was able to be home with my two daughters and visited with others at the same time. I shared my miniscule income with the girls as they always walked with me to deliver the collected news to an employee of the paper. I resigned after seven years when I began substitute teaching.

* * *

My two year old grandson, Shawn, was spending a week with me while his parents went to auto races in New York State. Olive, a friend, had asked me to accompany her to Washington Square, east of Indianapolis, Indiana on Highway 40 to return a purchase. As she approach a railroad crossing on German Church Road, off highway 52, visibility to the left was obstructed by buildings along the rail road tracks. A train was approaching at the same time we were. I later learned that a witness reported that Olive had not stopped, but started to cross the tracks. The train caught the front bumper of her car and whirled it around, and then caught the back bumper, whirled it around again before the car was dropped on the roadway. I was the most seriously injured with a fractured neck, head laceration, broken right arm and was unconscious for over 12 hours. My grandson had a mild concussion. Olive did not approve the use of seat belts, so Shawn's car seat was not secured as it was meant to be.

Dale began again, "It's your own fault you got hurt. You should have stayed home where you belong. You don't deserve pain and suffering compensation." I had had it with his control and verbal abuse. Within the next six months I filed for a divorce, even though I knew that finding gainful employment in my fifties would be next to impossible and worried that even if I found work, wondered how long I'd be able to work. I felt I deserved to visit my friends and my family when the cost was reasonable. When we had traveled to Nebraska to visit my family, Dale would drive the 1,050 miles straight through without a break except for food and gas. I'd be exhausted before we arrived.

It took me years to recover from the trauma of the accident and the divorce. I continued to live in our home in Milroy for several months after the divorce. I was now physically challenged and contacted the Indiana Disabilities Program for assistance. The special test that I took showed skills in teaching and office work. I attended Ball State University, Muncie Indiana for a Master's Degree in Special Education—Learning Disabilities. My tuition was provided by the Indiana State Disabilities program. Grandson Shawn was identified as learning disabled. It seemed important to try to understand his problems. I planned to move to Nebraska, to teach in special education and to be nearer Mama as she was nearly 90. She passed away before I completed the degree requirements.

* * *

In 1982 I moved to Bloomington, Indiana to help my daughter, Ruth with her three young children after her husband left her. I found part-time work and helped with child care. Here my volunteerism continued: the Salvation Army Ladies Auxiliary (charter member); Big Sister/Big Brothers; WonderLab volunteer; mentor and mentor coordinator; and Retired Senior Volunteer Program (RSVP) which coordinated several programs including Hug-a-Bears for young children at the Bloomington Hospital Emergency Room. I added Hug-a-Bears to the Tapp Road Surgical Center, preemie hats for the special care nursery at the Bloomington Hospital, and knitted hats and lap robes for cancer patients.

With God' guidance and my guardian angels, I finally emerged from the long, painful metamorphosis in the wilderness. My dream of owning my own home and a sewing/alteration business has become a successful reality. Writing my autobiography has been a dream for over 15 years. The companion book, *Getty-up Whoa* has been started.

I am a happy, respected member of my community, Bloomington, Indiana, and equal status in Rush County, Indiana where I resided for 33 years and in my childhood community in Dundy County, Nebraska. With my business, my volunteering and God's help, I feel I have **made something of myself.**

ABOUT THE AUTHOR

I was born in Dundy County, Nebraska, daughter of Homesteaders. My education began in a one-room school in rural Dundy, County; and continued at

*Photo courtesy of
Pauline Caldwell*

Parks High School, Parks, Nebraska. I received a B S. from Sterling College, Sterling, Kansas, and a Masters from Ball State University, Muncie, Indiana

My working career began with teaching in one-room schools in Nebraska, and substituting in the consolidated schools in Rush County, Indiana Currently, I am professional seamstress.

My writing began with a weekly community news column for the *Rushville Republican* news paper, Rushville, Indiana My first book, a genealogy book, *My Pioneer Ancestors* was compiled and published in 1993. I am currently composing *Getty-Up Whoa,* recalling operating a farm with horse-drawn machinery, a companion book for *Dundy County Babe.* My home is in Bloomington, Indiana.